PROTECTING LIBRARY STAFF, USERS, COLLECTIONS, AND FACILITIES

A How-To-Do-It Manual

Pamela J. Cravey

HOW-TO-DO-IT MANUALS
FOR LIBRARIANS

NUMBER 103

NEAL-SCHUMAN PUBLISHERS, INC.
New York, London

Published by Neal-Schuman Publishers, Inc.
100 Varick Street
New York, NY 10013

The paper used in this publication meets the minimum requirements of American National Standard for Information Sciences—Permanence of Paper for Printed Library Materials, ANSI Z39.48–1992.

Printed and bound in the United States of America.

ISBN 1–55570–392–5

Library of Congress Cataloging-in-Publication Data

Cravey, Pamela J.
    Protecting library staff, users, collections, and facilities : a how-to-do-it manual / Pamela J. Cravey.
        p. cm. — (How-to-do-it manuals for librarians ; no. 103)
    Includes bibliographical references.
    ISBN 1–55570–392–5 (alk. paper)
    1. Libraries—Safety measures—Handbooks, manuals, etc. 2. Library materials—Conservation and restoration—Handbooks, manuals, etc. 3. Disaster relief—Planning—Handbooks, manuals, etc. 4. Library planning—Handbooks, manuals, etc. I. Title. II. How-to-do-it manuals for libraries ; no. 103.

Z679.7 .C73 2001
025.8'2—dc 21
                                                                00–051123

CONTENTS

List of Figures   v
Preface   vii

Chapter 1 Library Security Today: An Overview   1
  Scope of Library Security   1
  Security Audit   11
  Example Security Audit Final Report   17
  Presentation of Survey Results   21
  Summary   22
  References   24

Chapter 2 Security of the General Collection   27
  Problems   27
  Definitions   29
  Loss and Mutilation Rates   32
  Cost of the Losses   34
  Developing a Proposal   34
  Types of Solutions   39
  Summary   47
  References   48

Chapter 3 Security of Users and Employees   51
  Expectations of a Safe Environment   51
  Building Security   53
  Personal Safety   58
  Types of Solutions   66
  Summary   76
  References   77

Chapter 4 Security of Electronic Files and Systems   79
  Fundamentals of Electronic Security   79
  Library-Specific Concerns   82
  Library-Specific Solutions   87
  Summary   101
  References   102

Chapter 5 Security of Special Collections   105
    Problem Described   105
    Solutions   109
    Summary   120
    References   121

Chapter 6 Security for Special Events   123
    An Overview of Planning   123
    The Security Plan   126
    Summary   127
    References   129

**Chapter 7 Library Security: Legal, Personnel, and
             Vendor Considerations**   131
    Legal Issues Related to Library Security   131
    Personnel Issues Related to Library Security   150
    Security Consultant and Vendor Selection Issues   157
    Summary   160
    References   162

Conclusion   165
    References   169

Index   171
About the Author   175

LIST OF FIGURES

Figure 1.1	Presentation of Survey Results	22
Figure 3.1	Inclusive Policy Statement	67
Figure 3.2	Disclaimer Statement	69
Figure 3.3	Draft Workplace Violence Policy	71
Figure 4.1	Sample Identification Log	90
Figure 4.2	Sample Risk Management Plan	95
Figure 4.3	Sample Corporate Security Policy	96
Figure 4.4	Sample Inclusive System Security Policy Statement	97
Figure 4.5	Sample Exclusive System Security Policy Statement	97
Figure 4.6	Sample Technical Security Policy	98
Figure 4.7	Sample Policy Standard Statement	98
Figure 4.8	Sample Policy and Standards Agreement Statement	100
Figure 7.1	Sample General Security Statement	135
Figure 7.2	Sample Specific Policy Statement	135
Figure 7.3	Sample Generic Legal Statement	138
Figure 7.4	Sample Specific Legal Statement	141
Figure 7.5	Buffered Narrative Report #1	144
Figure 7.6	Buffered Narrative Report #2	144
Figure 7.7	Sample Inappropriate Report Text	145
Figure 7.8	Unsuccessful Searcher's Report	145
Figure 7.9	Successful Searcher's Report	146
Figure 7.10	Sample Cover Letter	148
Figure 7.11	Sample Processing Steps Checklist	149
Figure 7.12	Sample Outcomes Checklist	149

PREFACE

Protecting Library Staff, Users, Collections, and Facilities: A How-To-Do-It Manual examines security for all types and sizes of libraries. Written from my perspective as a librarian and front-line library security officer, this book brings to bear many years of experience in developing and implementing an evolving security program. I have been involved in designing a security audit, writing a security plan, and developing policies and procedures for security. I have selected security systems, trained employees in security protocol, conducted workshops, and delivered national and regional presentations on a variety of security topics.

Most of my career has been engaged in thinking about security for libraries. I have worked with academic deans, university administrators, police, lawyers, county solicitors, judges, prosecutors, and defense attorneys. I have testified in court, written hundreds of incident reports, and ridden in police cruisers. I wrote *Protecting Library Staff, Users, Collections, and Facilities* when I realized that little in library education or continuing education classes prepares a professional to effectively design or implement a security program for their library. I hope this book will fill that need.

Attacks on library staff, theft of library materials, and vandalism of library property are all on the rise. These attacks undermine the building and its contents, impact service-delivery systems, and erode the spirit of library employees and users alike. An increase in reported abusive transactions with staff has undermined the sense of personal security of library employees. In addition, library users feel uneasy in the stacks, rest rooms, and in quiet areas of the libraries. The library has lost its status as a haven for quiet study. Our buildings, collections, and staffs are often caught in the middle of this issue.

Reasons for the rise of strengthening library security certainly have their roots in the broader social climate. Specific problems may evolve out of any number of reasons, including, but not limited to:

- Increase in societal aggression and violence
- Lessening sense of personal responsibility
- Behavioral shift in user expectations
- Change in how we relate to "public" institutions
- Climate of entitlement
- Children with little parental supervision
- Parents with only a slight sense of parental responsibility
- Increase in documented work-place violence

- Increase in gang activity
- Harassment
- Increase in the homeless population
- Long service hours with skeleton staffing
- Location of buildings in busy urban areas or in remote rural areas
- Perception of casualness.

Any administrator knows that there is a difference between alleviating a symptom and truly solving a problem. Band-Aid approaches and patches to specific incidents may help for the moment, but will not be effective over the long-term. Thus *Protecting Library Staff, Users, Collections, and Facilities: A How-To-Do-It Manual* approaches library security as a process rather than as a specific event. Each of the following seven chapters covers a specific portion of that process.

CHAPTER 1: LIBRARY SECURITY TODAY: AN OVERVIEW

Chapter 1 focuses on the scope of security issues. Several ways of organizing the variety of elements that combine to create a secure environment are highlighted to demonstrate the magnitude of the topic and see the scope of security issues.

The process of developing a comprehensive security plan begins with a security audit. Like an environmental scan, the security audit is an evaluation of all areas impacting security for a library. It forces broad thinking about the overall picture for a specific library. Chapter 1 covers the practical aspects of performing a security audit, the steps needed to prepare a final report and also features several examples of outlines for a security audit.

CHAPTER 2: SECURITY OF THE GENERAL COLLECTION

The term "general collection" is understood to mean those items, usually in open stacks, that are available for use in a self-service mode. Depending on the library, this definition could encompass books, periodicals, microforms, reserves, media, and reference items. How much security is necessary for the general collection? Planning for the answer to this question requires analyzing current loss and mutilation rates. Variation in loss and mutilation rates over the years provides excellent documentation for any security proposal. Once the rates are available, the cost of these losses can be calculated. Help for determining costs is included in the chapter. Types of security solutions are also presented. Solutions, ranging from low-intensity to high-intensity, are enumerated. The chapter ends with a list of elements comprising a security proposal.

CHAPTER 3: SECURITY OF USERS AND EMPLOYEES

Users will be reluctant to come to the library if they think it is unsafe. Administrative lip service frequently is given to the idea that people do not have a right to threaten or abuse library users or employees. In reality, this abuse occurs daily.

While librarians can probably do little to erase the growing fear of public places, something can be done about safety and security in and around the library. Chapter 3 begins with an explanation of an environmental scan as a planning tool. It concludes with examples of measures that can enhance both the perception and the reality of the library as a safe haven.

CHAPTER 4: SECURITY OF ELECTRONIC FILES AND SYSTEMS

Chapter 4 is devoted to protecting the electronic systems, files, and equipment that exist in today's libraries. Issues addressed include: How can libraries offer ease of access for their users while still securing various systems? How can ease of access and security be tied to licensing agreements? How can we secure electronic files and systems that can become dated as soon as the latest software package is released?

The first part of Chapter 4 introduces computer security terms. Painting with a broad brush, it explains topics, and then refers interested readers to other texts which address these topics in detail. The second part of the chapter introduces the risk analysis/management process as a means to establish an electronic security program for libraries. Security of the digital library can be as comprehensive or as limited as the library needs or can afford. The last part of this chapter suggests solutions spanning the range of personal invasiveness, cost, and aggression for tackling various security concerns.

CHAPTER 5: SECURITY OF SPECIAL COLLECTIONS

Since we now view security as a holistic process, the security of special collections is not very different from the process of securing other parts of the library. When differences occur, they are mostly in magnitude. Chapter 5 briefly identifies some of the unique problems and solutions associated with protecting special collections. Collaboration with other groups and archives, and development of training programs are introduced as important aspects of all security plans. These are especially important elements in planning security for special collections.

CHAPTER 6: SECURITY FOR SPECIAL EVENTS

Chapter 6 of this book deals with security issues for major special events. While most librarians may not need to prepare for massive public events being held outside their library's door, most librarians do have to consider special security concerns. Events associated with local political, musical, festival, or sporting events will affect traffic and service patterns around, and possibly in, your library.

CHAPTER 7: LIBRARY SECURITY: LEGAL, PERSONNEL, AND VENDOR CONSIDERATIONS

Security is a complex matter, driven by local laws and ordinances. In fact, legal definitions and consequences may vary by jurisdiction. To have an overall security plan with any "teeth" requires close collaboration with local legal and enforcement units involved with the library.

For example, one academic library began its security program with an electronic book-theft detection system to stop theft of materials from the general collection. Soon, the library decided to prosecute people caught in the system who were trying to steal library items. This library worked as a team with campus officials (administrators, lawyers, and police) and the office of the county solicitor. Collaborating from the beginning with such a high-level team, the library was able to develop a program with solid legal footing. This program encompassed:

- Arresting people caught trying to steal library materials
- Providing appropriate legal representation for staff who were involved in carrying out the procedures
- Treating all suspects equally
- Handling and processing evidence with legally appropriate procedures
- Maintaining a paper trail that satisfied all legal units
- Mandating specific language to be used consistently
- Defining terms with legally approved definitions.

This well-developed program convinced involved library staff and others that the library was serious about security. Further, staff believed administrators would do whatever was necessary to support them in the implementation of the procedures. Word quickly spread that people were being arrested for stealing library materials. The number of incidents at the electronic exit gate diminished. Soon judges hearing the cases realized how large the theft problem was at the library and began to administer realistic sentences that addressed the problem. A program like this one could not have been successful without the cooperation and understanding of the local police and legal representatives.

Even if a library does not plan to take such a serious stand on security, advice and approval from legal and enforcement units is critical to the success of the program. This last chapter includes information on and examples of internal documentation, policies, procedures, and some personnel matters that are related to library security and the law. The chapter also addresses security consultant and vendor selection issues.

Just as new security problems are introduced into our culture, security solutions continue to emerge. As librarians review and adapt the literature of other disciplines, such as systems theory in sociology, new solutions become apparent. The field of librarianship also has to undergo a shift in professional ethos to one of continuing to serve our public while also serving our collections, staff, and users. *Protecting Library Staff, Users, Collections, and Facilities: A How-To-Do-It Manual* presents security as one essential element of the library's overall service package.

1 LIBRARY SECURITY TODAY: AN OVERVIEW

SCOPE OF LIBRARY SECURITY

The "big picture" of library security can be enormous. While specific security concerns vary by size and type of library, all libraries must deal with security. Security matters influence all aspects of library operations. Ideally, security issues will have been addressed before the building was designed, before the site was surveyed and before renovation projects were begun. In reality, however, security is a reactive sport. That is, as problems are identified, solutions are sought. A systematic, proactive approach to security results in better security—even if security is being addressed retrospectively.

Before specific library security measures can be implemented, a decision must be made about how much security is needed. Does the library need an electronic book-theft detection system? Does the library need police guards? These questions and others cannot adequately be answered without some type of formal security plan. There are many ways to organize thinking about library security in order to arrive at such a plan. A systematic look at the scope of security, followed by the completion of a security audit, should lead to the development of a relevant security plan. Getting a handle on the scope of library security issues is the first step toward a planned approach to identifying and meeting each library's individual security needs.

The scope of security for any type of library includes many overall areas. "When a library staff becomes security conscious, an almost infinite list of security issues or concerns can be developed." (Shaughnessy, 1984: 22) Elements to consider in a systematic approach to security issues can be organized in many different ways. The following sections provide some examples of ways security issues can be categorized. They also highlight the breadth of topics found under the security umbrella.

RESULTS CLUSTERS

One systematic way to characterize security issues is by results clusters. Results clusters look at the end result of security measures. The results clusters identified below include physical security, security of staff and users, security from natural disasters, and security of information. There is nothing magical about these cluster headings or about the elements listed under them. They were gleaned from the literature. First, a content analysis of twenty years' worth of library readings on security was used to develop a comprehensive list of security-related topics. Then, the topics were grouped into thematic clusters. Four clusters emerged. These four clusters are designed to illuminate the scope of topics related to security.

Physical Security

Physical security refers to elements related to the building and its design or operation. This cluster often includes the following elements:

- Site selection
- Neighborhood
- Boundaries
- Building design
- Parking lot design and location
- Sidewalks
- Access pathways
- External lighting (including in parking lots)
- Landscaping
- Fencing
- Design of the main entrance
- Wheelchair access
- Type of front doors
- Type of interior doors
- Lobby security
- Design of stairwells and handrails
- Use of glass
- Internal lighting
- Emergency lighting
- Emergency stairwells
- Walls
- Fire doors
- Locks and keying
- Elevators
- Rest rooms
- Sign systems (including Braille)
- Book returns
- Audible, inaudible, and flashing alarm systems
- Evacuation plans
- Broken windows
- Graffiti

Security of Staff and Users

Security of staff and users refers to people, where they are, and library policies that dictate their movement. This cluster can include the following themes:

- Access management
- Service hours
- Study hours
- Clientele served
- Who is in the building and when
- Library policies
- Patrols
- Availability of escort services
- Position of the stacks relative to staffed areas
- Shelving systems
- Open/closed stacks
- Location of isolated areas
- Where money is collected
- Presence of CCTV (Closed Circuit Television)
- Problem patrons
- Assaults
- Hostage situations
- Illegal sexual activity
- Presence of gangs
- Theft of personal property
- Crimes of opportunity
- Vagrants
- Verbal threats
- Voyeurism/exhibitionism
- Screening incoming telephone calls
- Personnel policies
- Policies regarding employee termination
- Preemployment screening

Security from Natural Disasters

Fortunately, most libraries do not have to deal with natural disasters very often. As a result, policies and procedures related to them have to be thoroughly documented and posted where staff can quickly find them during all hours of operation. These procedures should include a list of important telephone numbers to call to alert institutional officials to problems after normal business hours. An excellent tool for assisting in emergency responses is the *Emergency Response and Salvage Wheel*. (National Task Force on Emergency Response, 1997) This product provides suggestions for fast responses to many disasters and provides a place for appropriate emergency telephone numbers to be noted. The *Library Disaster Planning and Recovery Handbook* (Alire, 2000) documents the efforts of the Colorado State University Library to recover from a disastrous flood. By recording the steps performed to restore the library and its services, they created a landmark compilation of practical suggestions for dealing with natural disasters. Natural disasters can include the following:

- Earthquake
- Fire
- Flood
- Hurricane
- Tornado
- Vermin
- Wind damage

Security of Information

Many library users think breaches of security of information are the most insidious security violations of all. Usually security violations of this sort result in the loss of some information. Security of information can include the following topics:

- Computer trespassing
- Food, drink, smoke
- Mutilation
- Photocopy cost
- Availability of change machines
- Photocopy policy
- Location of and condition of copiers
- Procedures for using special and rare collections
- Security of equipment
- Security of audiovisual materials
- Security of nonprint materials
- Theft

ALTERNATE WAYS TO ORGANIZE SECURITY CONSIDERATIONS

Security considerations do not have to be organized into results clusters. Similar and dissimilar collection security elements have been categorized in a variety of ways using a medley of groupings. Often the elements within each grouping are less comprehensive than the above lists but are more effective and more relevant for a particular library. This section includes examples of other ways security issues have been categorized by various authors from several disciplines.

Emergency Planner

Trinity University Library looked at security as a response to emergencies. The result is a comprehensive procedural manual for identifying and responding to various types of emergencies that are important

to the organization. (Pettit, 1981: 6–7) In the process of developing this emergency planner, areas of concern were also grouped into four categories. However, the four selected categories are different from those identified in the preceding results clusters. The emergency planning categories identified by Trinity University Library are:

- Behavioral emergencies
  — Building takeovers
  — Bomb threats
  — Problem patrons
  — Thefts
- Building emergencies
  — Elevator failure
  — Fire
  — Flooding of building
  — Water leaks
  — Power failure
- Medical emergencies
  — Animal bites
  — Death
  — Drug or psychiatric problems
  — Fumes
  — Medical problems
  — Injuries
  — Insect stings
- Weather emergencies
  — Heavy rain
  — Icy conditions
  — Tornadoes

Catalyst for Program Development

Campus Crime Prevention Programs (CCPP) developed a comprehensive manual "to address the unique safety, security and patron management problems related to libraries. . . ." (Campus Crime Prevention Programs, 1992: iii) This manual divides the inventory of related security issues into "major" and "minor" problems. These problems are further categorized as either "natural," "man-made," or "accidental." (Campus Crime Prevention, 1992: 107–108) The following is a list of CCPP's security-related inventory to be used as a catalyst for developing a program for building and staff readiness.

- Major natural disasters
  — Tornado
  — Earthquake
  — Hurricane
  — Flood

- — Snow or other adverse weather
- Major man-made disasters that occur because of an intentional act
  - — Bombs or bomb threats
  - — Nuclear war
  - — Building occupations/civil disturbances
  - — Major work stoppage
- Major accidental emergencies that result from an unintentional act
  - — Fire
  - — Explosion
  - — Chemical spill
  - — Gas leaks
  - — Extended power outages
  - — Water damage and leaks
  - — Toxic fumes or substances
- Minor natural emergencies that have a limited potential for serious disruption of library activities
  - — Illness
  - — Insect bites
  - — Animal bites
- Minor man-made emergencies that usually only affect a small portion of the building or its occupants
  - — Theft or vandalism
  - — Book-theft alarm
  - — Violent patrons
  - — Disorderly or harassing patrons
  - — Patrons with obvious mental problems
  - — Alcohol or drug problems
  - — Sexual misconduct
  - — Malicious false alarms
- Minor accidental situations
  - — Personal injury
  - — Stuck elevators
  - — Environmental system failure
  - — A lost child
  - — Accidental fire alarm

Training Checklist

Approaching the identification of library security concerns as a checklist for an in-service training program, Paris (1984: 81–82) identified six categories to consider. The result is a list specifically designed to be used and modified by all types of libraries. Though dated, Paris's categorization is unusual because it combines policies, inspection tours, responsibilities, and emergencies in one list. The training checklist includes the following:

- Written security policies and procedures
  - Library handbooks and manuals
  - Library floor layouts
  - Security for campus, city, county, etc.
- Tour of interior and exterior physical facilities
  - Emergency exits
  - Parking facilities
  - Lighting systems
  - Fire alarms
  - Emergency telephones
  - Ingress and egress
  - Rest room security
  - Collections requiring special security
  - Secluded areas
- Equipment, devices, protection measures
  - Door locks
  - Alarm signals
  - Intercoms
  - Fire extinguishers
  - Electronic security/detection systems
  - First-aid kits
  - Automatic signaling devices
  - Pagers, walkie-talkies
  - Window locks
  - Money handling
  - Central control consoles
  - CCTV
- Major security problems and procedures
  - Theft
  - Mutilation
  - Non-return of materials
  - Arson
  - Disruptive patrons
  - Medical emergencies
  - Power outages
  - Bomb threats
  - Fires
  - Floods
  - Storms
- Staff's responsibilities
  - To each other
  - To the patrons
  - To the collections

- Auxiliary personnel
  - Security guards
  - City or campus police
  - Fire department
  - Paramedics
  - Mental health and social workers
  - Legal advisors

Response to Crime

In a landmark survey of libraries, Lincoln, a criminologist, used five topics to delineate security concerns. (Lincoln, 1984b: 70–79) These topics are:

- Vandalism
  - Intentional book damage
  - Damage to cars in the parking lots
  - Damage to equipment
- Arson
- Theft
- Assault
- Problem patrons
  - Verbal abuse of the staff or patrons
  - Drug use or sales
  - Indecent exposure

A Systems Approach

Kingsbury (1979: 5–6) also advocates completing a topical list as a first step in the security audit process. Writing from the business perspective, he designed a generic list to be used in categorizing security issues in all types of businesses and organizations—public and private. While stressing the importance of staying focused on the ideas of personal, physical, and informational security, he uses a systems approach to organize the topical outline into the following seven major areas of concentration:

- General organizational, geographic, demographic, and informational facts about the library, its history, budget, and officers
- Sociopolitical considerations
  - Community groups
  - Local power structures
  - Political factors of the community
  - Economic factors of the community
- Physical security
  - Perimeter barriers

- — Lighting
- — Alarms
- — Entrances
- • Security of people
  - — Security clearances
  - — Disaster and emergency plans
  - — Morale
- • Information security
- • Security education
- • Fire-fighting concerns

Survey

Using a checklist format for a survey of relevant security topics, Shaughnessy (1984: 22–23) provides an illustrative list of important concerns in seven different clusters. This list differs from the others, as it intentionally excludes natural disasters as security topics. Instead, disasters are thought of as different from security issues. Shaughnessy's security survey list encompasses:

- • Security of collections/equipment
  - — Electronic security systems
  - — Collection access policy
  - — Exit management, guards, attendants
  - — Publication of penalties
  - — Property stamps
  - — Ownership markings
  - — Up-to-date equipment inventory
  - — Storage lockers for equipment
  - — Vehicle security
  - — Accurate identification of users
  - — Accurate identification of borrowers
  - — After-use procedures for damage review
- • Security of cash
  - — Vending machines
  - — Change machines
  - — Access to coin boxes, cash registers
  - — Access to safes
  - — Cash handling procedures/accountability
- • Bibliographic and patron records
  - — Terminal access and permissions
  - — Passwords
  - — Backup devices (tape, disk, and others)
  - — Off-site location for backup data
  - — Microfilm duplication of records

- Personnel records
  — Access policy
  — Supervision of record examination
  — Use of logs to record access
  — Policy on confidential data/records
  — Secure storage
- Employee and patron security
  — Entrance/exit controls
  — Use of emergency exits
  — Building design/surveillance
  — Patrols or monitors
  — Building access policy
  — Staff ID badges
  — Emergency telephones
- Key policy and building security
  — Procedures for issuing/reclaiming keys
  — Periodic lock changes
  — Silent alarms
  — Parking lot security
  — Lighting
  — Custodial services access
  — Window security
  — Book drop security
- Other
  — Liability and other insurance issues
  — Legal counsel
  — Periodic meetings with the lawyer
  — Budget implications for security

An Approach Based on Vulnerabilities

Boss (1984) indicates that the typical library security "plan" has been a reaction to breaches of security. He further suggests that libraries need to shift from that approach to a proactive approach. Suggesting that libraries take a broad view of security, he groups policies and procedures into 11 areas of vulnerability that weaken library security. These areas are:

- Access
- Keys
- Exit control
- Unauthorized possession or occupancy
- Rules and statutes
- Property marking
- Loans and renewals
- Circulation systems

- Photocopying
- Terminations
- Security manuals

Questionnaire

A final way to look at security topics is through a questionnaire. As an independent business consultant, Harold (1989: 57–69) presents a series of questions about security. While these questions were not designed specifically for libraries, the straightforward format makes them applicable to all types of libraries and media centers. The questions cluster under the following headings:

- Site survey and risk assessment
- Physical security
- Security of the physical plant
- Guard security
- Office security

It should be clear from these examples of alternate ways to organize security considerations that a comprehensive list could be endless. It should also be clear that there is no single correct way to view the scope of security. For some libraries a security list would overlap with an emergency or disaster list. In other libraries these topics would be viewed separately. (Elder, 1986: 1–10) The key to understanding the scope of security is that it must reflect the unique needs of each organization.

SECURITY AUDIT

The above lists and groupings of elements illuminate the broad scope of security issues related to libraries. The issues cited and others that are relevant to each individual library should be considered when developing a security audit. Staff surveys, paper and electronic user surveys, focus groups, and the like can be used to detect issues important to a particular library. There is no correct list and there are no correct groupings. However, no matter how the issues related to library security are viewed, the best way to begin honing in on security issues that are important to an individual library is with a security audit. In the following sections, security audits are described and illustrated.

DESCRIPTION OF A SECURITY AUDIT

A security audit "is a critical on-site examination and analysis of an industrial plant, business, home, public or private institution, to ascertain the present security status, to identify deficiencies or excesses, to determine the protection needed, and to make recommendations to improve the over-all security." (Kingsbury, 1979: 2–4) It is like an environmental scan, but its focus is exclusively on security. A security audit may include consideration of risk management factors such as insurance, comments about environmental and personal security issues, results of an analysis of crime patterns, and thoughts about uncomfortable topics such as fraud and internal theft. An analysis of the building's floor plans may be important. On these plans, specific areas of vulnerability could be noted. A security audit could also include a statement on the personality of the building. (Fennelly, 1989: 48–49)

Security audits can be formal and extensive or they can be in the format of a general checklist. Libraries can design and use their own audit, adapt an existing document, or engage a variety of internal or external helpers (task forces or ad hoc committees) to create and complete the audit. Several commercial ventures will conduct a library security audit for a fee. (Layne, 1994a: 46–47) Vendors of security equipment will usually conduct a security audit in areas specific to the equipment they sell. Vendor audits may be offered at no cost, at low cost, or as part of a deal to reduce the subsequent purchase price of their equipment. Also, consultants can be hired to work independently or with an institutional group. A parent organization might fund the audit or the library might fund it. The Friends of the Library group might be interested in raising money to support a professional security audit, or a class of alumni might want to donate the audit as part of a class gift. Once the final security audit report is completed, that same group might also be interested in targeting specific elements to support in a capital campaign.

EXAMPLES OF SECURITY AUDITS

Good examples of elements in generic security audits can be found in Kingsbury (1979: 2–4), Lincoln (1984a: 156–158), Paris (1984: 80–82), and Layne (1994a: 11–12; 1994b: [7]). Paris's (1984: 51–80) discussion of security audits, though dated, also pays particular attention to the differences in audits for school, university, and public libraries. While the importance of an audit spans all types of libraries, the specific topics of interest vary. An example of an institution-specific audit can be found for Cornell University. (Currie et al., 1985: 3–13) Other university library audits can be found in various Association of Research Libraries—Office of Management Studies—Systems and Procedures Exchange Center publications.

Boss (1984: 44–46) suggests that a traditional and generic security audit might conform to the following outline.

I. Nature of the community, campus, organization
   A. General description
   B. Size
   C. Degree of isolation
   D. Prominence of the collections
   E. Attitudes of staff and users
II. Indicators of security weaknesses
   A. Evidence of theft
      1. Complaints
      2. Collection count
      3. Inventory
      4. Random sampling
   B. Evidence of vandalism, including mutilation
   C. Patterns of past losses
   D. Existence of valuable special collections
   E. Vulnerability of building
   F. Lack of policy for keys
   G. Lack of written closing procedures
   H. Lack of an unauthorized possession policy
   I. Lack of an occupancy policy
   J. Lack of written access policy
   K. Inflexible loan policy
   L. Inflexible renewal policy
   M. Lack of written termination procedures
      1. Employees
      2. Patrons
   N. Limited property marking
   O. No participation in theft alerting clearing houses
III. Observation of present security points
   A. Principal exit(s)
      1. Location(s) necessary
      2. Security system installed
         a. Full-circulating
         b. By-pass
      3. Guards
         a. Full search
         b. Random search
         c. Casual
         d. Purses checked
      4. Restricted flow
      5. Patron behavior
      6. Characteristics of doors and locks

B. Emergency exit(s)
   1. Visual control
   2. Alarm
   3. Electronic recording
   4. Characteristics of doors and locks
C. Employee exit(s)
   1. Visual control
   2. Staffed
   3. Locked
   4. Characteristics of doors and locks
D. Loading dock
   1. Visual control
   2. Staffed
   3. Locked
   4. Characteristics of doors and locks
E. Windows
   1. Locked
   2. Secured with screens
   3. Alarm
   4. Ease of breakage
F. Utility tunnel(s)
   1. Locked
   2. Exits
G. Ceiling type
   1. Access to security system
   2. Crawl space
H. After-hours concealment
   1. Ease of concealment
   2. Ease of exit
I. Special collections
   1. Locked
   2. Alarm
   3. Characteristics of doors, windows
   4. Characteristics of ceilings
   5. Ease of concealment
   6. Ease of exit
J. Exhibit cases
   1. Secure
   2. Alarm
K. After-hours book return
   1. Capacity
   2. Ease of removal
   3. Ease of vandalism/arson
L. Smoke/fire detectors
   1. Adequate number

2. Reachable
3. Evidence of damage or poor maintenance
4. Ease of false alarm

M. Computer room
1. Staffed
2. Locked
3. Availability of key
4. Backup for files kept off-site
5. Fire detection
6. Automatic fire extinguishing
7. Use of passwords and access controls
8. Audit trails for record changes

Just as it is clear that the list of topics under the security audit umbrella is enormous, it should now be clear that there is a lot of variation in the elements included in a security audit. The most important idea for a security audit is that it needs to result in a document that leads to an individualized plan for each specific library.

DEVELOPING A SECURITY AUDIT: NUTS AND BOLTS

This section lists a series of steps to consider in performing a formal security audit for your library.

- Appoint a committee or task force to complete the audit and its final report. Have wide representation from all library departments.
- Survey library employees anonymously. Ask employees to list, in detail, the security concerns they have.
- Consider surveying users. Security issues are important to users. Often users bring to a survey a perspective library staff cannot know. Consider the usual survey options. Focus groups also provide an easy way for users to divulge information.
- Analyze all survey responses. Three or four dominant themes will probably emerge from the surveys. If possible, group the majority of the responses into these themes. Include the complete, unedited list of responses as an appendix in the final report.
- Research the themes. Divide the task force into subcommittees, and research each of the identified themes.
- Prepare a formal background report about each theme. Include these formal topical reports as appendixes in the final report. Remember, the committee now knows more about these topics than other readers. Use the reports as an opportunity to bring others "up to speed."

- Discuss recommendations. Staff and user concerns should form the basis of these discussions. Turn the discussions into specific appropriate recommendations for each thematic area. These recommendations become a major part of the final report.
- Consider other recommendations. Do not limit your recommendations to elements that only address concerns of the staff and users. Rather, include items the task force, after completing its extensive research on each topic, deems important.
- Plan the final report. One logical way to present your final recommendations is by theme. Begin your report by naming the first theme and present your recommendations relating to that theme. Name your second theme and list related recommendations, and so forth. Themes can be listed alphabetically or by perceived importance. There are also other ways to present findings. Explore the alternatives and select the format that best represents your library's needs.
- Plan for the format of the final report. In terms of catching the eye of the reader and the funding sources, the layout of the report may be as important as the contents. Consequently, decisions will have to be made about what is to go in the front matter, the body, and the appendixes. For example, the following order could be useful:
  — The charge
  — Recommendations
  — The unedited survey responses as an appendix
  — The background reports as an appendix
  — References
- To simplify group discussion of the final document, recommendations should be consecutively numbered or the line numbers from the draft should remain in the final report.
- Consider additional and alternative presentations of the same information. Be sure to include the recommendation number or the line number in the presentation of information in additional or alternate ways. For example, divide recommendations into the following categories:
  — Things that could be done now
  — Things that could be done with a small effort/cost
  — Things that could be done with a medium effort/cost
  — Things that would require a large effort or cost

EXAMPLE SECURITY AUDIT FINAL REPORT

Following is an example of the final report from a security audit. The example includes a narrative framework for the final report and some illustrative recommendations. To improve readability, suggestions for crafting each section of the report are presented in brackets. Use of the words "other" and "another" indicates the list could go on from the few suggestions made. Again, all recommendations should be specific to your institution and will not necessarily be important to other institutions.

CHARGE TO THE TASK FORCE

The Task Force on Library Safety and Security, comprising one member from each department of the Shining Arrow Public Library, was created on July 1, 2000, and charged with the following responsibilities:

- Identification of security issues important to the library
- Recommendation of strategies for addressing them
- Other

RECOMMENDATIONS

[This section would include the all-encompassing list of recommendations from the task force. For this example, the recommendations section of the final report is organized with topical headings. A brief summary of the topic grounded in the literature from the research reports, and the specific recommendations in list form follow.]

General Introduction to the Report

[Since the report is tied specifically to the literature of general security, as well as to that specific to library security, a summary of important findings is presented at the beginning of the report. An example of a general introduction follows.]

According to *Crime in the Library* (Lincoln, 1984a) there is a high correlation between the amount of crime in a library and the following characteristics:

- Size of the city
- Location within the city
- Age of the clientele
- Number of people entering the library daily
- Number of service hours

Additionally, libraries possess unique characteristics not found in many other institutions. These characteristics include:

- Open-door policy
- Users not monitored by library personnel
- Users engrossed in their own work and not always alert to goings-on around them
- Maze-like physical layout
- Many hidden corners and isolated reading areas

Of these high-risk characteristics, the Shining Arrow Public Library is characterized by the following:

- Location in large urban area
- Location in high-crime area
- Large population in the 18–22 age range
- Service to an average of approximately 7,000 people per day
- Other

In recognition of the environmental factors that impinge on our ability to provide a safe facility for users and employees, the Task Force on Library Safety and Security makes the following specific recommendations:

Specific Recommendations

A. Exterior of the building [This is the topical heading. It is followed by a brief paragraph about the topic—grounded in the literature—and then by the list of specific recommendations related to the topic. See section B below for an example of the wording.]

1. Paths to parking should be lighted. [The actual recommendations should include details about each item. For example, instead of saying "Paths to parking should be lighted," the actual report should recommend which paths should be lighted, how many more lights should be added, what fixtures should be repaired or moved, and so forth.]
2. Lights should be on after dark.
3. Provide freestanding exterior book drops.
4. Book drops should be bomb proof.
5. Other.

B. Entrance/exit management [In one sample report, the introductory paragraph stated: "Crime would be reduced if we could control access to the library. We cannot prevent anyone from coming in to use the library, nor do we want to inhibit patrons who have legitimate library needs, but we could identify those who enter the buildings. Entrance/exit management would go a long way to enhancing the security of the library." (Georgia State University, 1997) A similar statement should precede each heading.]

6. Hire personnel for this task.
7. Require all affiliated persons to show ID.
8. Initiate visitor log and require photo ID.
9. Require employees and visitors to wear ID.
10. Limit number of entrance points.
11. Use time-lapse video for entrances.
12. Suspend night cleaning.
13. Change external locks and restrict keys.
14. Hire people to help clear the building.
15. Other.

C. Collections [Use an introductory paragraph about collections, such as the example in the previous section.]

16. Support collection security policy.
17. Other.

D. Money

18. Continue stringent desk money management.
19. Centralize money collection at one desk.
20. Other.

E. Equipment

21. Identify equipment manager for all areas.
22. Inventory equipment regularly.
23. Use lockable bins to store loose items.
24. Other.

F. People

25. Use electronic access management system.
26a. Teach appropriate "challenging skills."
26b. Use these skills to identify unfamiliar people in office areas.
27. Require employees to wear visible badges.
28. Appoint a library safety officer.
29. File a safety report for all incidents.
30. Use this form to identify trends.
31. Hire personnel to patrol the library.
32. Provide direct police phones.

33. Give a beeper to staff in some areas.
34. Provide portable video monitors.
35. Install cameras at service desks.
36. Install locks on staff desks.
37. Assign staff lockers for personal items.
38. Other.

G. Police

39. Strengthen relationship with police.
40. Meet officer trainees.
41. Enhance police visibility.
42. Have continuous building patrols.
43. Create a police substation in library.
44. Other.

H. Training

45. Train personnel how to react in specific situations, such as:
    - For theft and mutilation of all types of library materials
    - To a variety of deviants, like peepers, self-fondlers, and people who follow others through the stack areas
    - Verbal, gender, or other forms of harassment
    - Strategies to avoid becoming a victim of a variety of offenses
    - Administrative and public service procedures to follow in case any specific crime has been committed
    - Policies that may help deter crime
    - Inappropriate and aberrant behavior in elevators
46. Train users to deal with the same specific situations.
47. Train persons from other departments (custodial) in the above situations and in:
    - After-hours security
    - Food policies
    - Light policies
    - Temperature-range policies
    - Humidity policies
48. Instruct police in all of the above.
49. Other.

I. Disaster preparedness

50. Hire professional to do risk analysis.
51. Develop a plan to address bomb threats.
52. Develop a safety plan for opening mail.
53. Develop a plan to address other threats.
54. Other.

J. Unacceptable behavior

55a. Identify unacceptable behaviors.
55b. Develop procedures for recognizing, teaching about, and dealing with them.
56. Provide staff training for what to do when discovering unacceptable behavior [specific behaviors named].
57. Develop a food and drink policy.
58. Develop training to assure compliance with institution's discriminatory harassment policy and other relevant policies.
59. Other.

K. Data

60. Develop a security policy for electronic data and files used in the library.
61. If affordable, conduct a network risk analysis.
62. Other.

L. Other.

REFERENCES CITED
[Since this report is literature-based, cite the references used. Include references only if they are cited in the final reports.]

APPENDIXES
[This section includes the original list of staff concerns and the individual topical background reports. Include these items especially if you do not make a recommendation about every point raised. Also, include the results of the various surveys.]

PRESENTATION OF SURVEY RESULTS

One appendix should include the summary of the survey results as an introduction to the presentation of the raw survey data. Figure 1.1 is an example of the way survey results can be summarized.

INTRODUCTION TO PRESENTATION
Included in the introduction should be information about the survey respondents, the survey instrument, the way the results were tabulated, and other pertinent information about the presentation.

**Figure 1.1: Presentation of Survey Results
Shining Arrow Public Library**

Members of the Shining Arrow Public Library staff were surveyed with an anonymous and open-ended questionnaire form. 150 employees, including librarians, support staff, and pages received such survey instruments. The purpose of the survey was to determine the scope of security concerns among library employees. 112 responses were received for a response rate of approximately 75%. Because the survey was designed to be anonymous, responses were not tabulated by rank. Concerns of the surveyed group could be categorized into seven categories. These categories and the specific concerns expressed included:

Personal safety
Security of equipment
Security of materials
Security of data
Security of the building
Other identified categories

Within each of the above categories, this report will present the employee concerns in order of frequency cited.

PRESENTATION OF FINDINGS

In this section should be the presentation of findings in the format selected by the committee. The findings could be grouped first by topical main heading. Under each main heading would be the display of concerns uncovered by the survey. Such a display could be in list form—arranged alphabetically by topic, in order of frequency mentioned, or in any other specified arrangement. The display also could be in the form of a graph, chart, or any other easy-to-read format.

SUMMARY

There are many benefits to be gained from participating in a security audit process. According to Layne (1977: 50–51), from a security audit can come such benefits as:

- Guidelines for long-term and short-term planning for security
- Guidelines for allocation of budget resources to security issues
- Reviews of policies and procedures about security, emergency and disaster preparedness, personnel, harassment, drugs, and related issues

In addition to these administrative benefits of completing a security audit, there are other benefits, as well. For example, if a contracted firm is used, the audit will be completed in a timely fashion. If a vendor audit is selected, it will focus on a specific issue and may lead to future price reductions in sales. If stakeholders, such as a Friends group, are convinced to support the audit, their support will be invaluable in the subsequent implementation and funding phases. If a library-wide team is selected to complete the security audit, the report will probably take longer to complete. However, if the members are chosen to represent all functions of library operations, an awareness of the concerns of coworkers can go a long way toward creating an unprecedented unity within the organization. A team-based audit will also stay focused on the issues of the organization rather than on a consultant's "formula" plan.

Lincoln (1984a: 155–156) summarizes the five stages in a crime-based model security program as:

- Devising a security checklist
- Making a risk assessment study
- Monitoring crime patterns
- Establishing a reporting procedure
- Implementing the program

Performing a security audit (risk management assessment) is critical. The advantages of such an audit are:

- Forcing the organization to review the universe of security issues
- Permitting the organization to think logically about specific issues related to its own security
- Resulting in a personalized security profile
- Leading toward the development of the security plan best suited for that unique facility and its clientele

Like most planning processes, the lengthy development of a security audit yields great rewards when it is complete. The success of the security audit is in the quality of the recommendations that follow. A security audit answers the question "How big is the 'big picture' in my library?"

REFERENCES

Alire, Camila, ed. 2000. *Library Disaster Planning and Recovery Handbook*. New York: Neal-Schuman.

Association of Research Libraries—Office of Management Studies—The Systems and Procedures Exchange Center. 1984–1989. *#100, Collection Security in ARL Libraries; #144, Building Use Policies*; and *#150, Building Security and Personal Safety*. Washington, D.C.: Association of Research Libraries, Office of Management Studies.

Boss, Richard W. 1984. "Collection Security." *Library Trends* 33, no. 1: 39–48.

Campus Crime Prevention Programs. 1992. *Library Safety and Security: A Comprehensive Manual for Library Administrators and Police and Security Officers*. Goshen, Ky.: Campus Crime Prevention Programs.

Currie, Susan, Howard Raskin, Samuel Demas, Kristine Kreilick, and Charles McNamara. 1985. "Cornell University Libraries' Security Checklist." *Library & Archival Security* 7, no. 2: 3–13.

Elder, James G. 1986. "Emergency Planning for College and University Libraries." In *Crime Prevention, Security and Emergency Procedures for University Libraries*. Louisville, Ky.: Campus Crime Prevention Programs.

Fennelly, Lawrence J. 1989. "Security Surveys." In *Handbook of Loss Prevention and Crime Prevention*, 2nd ed., edited by Lawrence J. Fennelly. Boston: Butterworths.

Georgia State University, William Russell Pullen Library. 1997. "Library Security: Task Force on Library Security Final Report." Unpublished working document. Atlanta. The Task Force consisted of one member from each library department. Members included David G. Anderson, Betina Coburn, Brian O. Gorman, Mary Jo Howard, Mary Kuck, Susan Moss, and Pamela J. Cravey, Chair. The elaborate final presentation matrix placing each recommendation into a cell was designed and compiled by Angela C. Clark.

Harold, Victor. 1989. Appendix 4a: "Site Survey and Risk Assessment"; Appendix 4b: "Physical Security Survey"; Appendix 4c: "Plant Security Checklist"; Appendix 4d: "Guard Security Checklist"; and Appendix 4e: "Office Security Checklist." In *Handbook of Loss Prevention and Crime Prevention*, 2d ed., edited by Lawrence J. Fennelly. Boston: Butterworths.

Kingsbury, Arthur A. 1979. "Security of Property and Person." In *Handbook of Building Security Planning and Design*, edited by Peter S. Hopf. New York: McGraw-Hill.

Layne, Stevan P. 1977. "Same Story . . . Different Day." *Library & Archival Security* 14, no. 1: 45–51.

————. 1994a. *The Official Library Security Manual.* Dillon, Co.: Layne Consultants International.

————. 1994b. "Risk Assessment." In *Violence in the Library: Prevention, Preparedness and Response.* Dillon, Co.: Layne Consultants International.

Lincoln, Alan Jay. 1984a. *Crime in the Library: A Study of Patterns, Impact, and Security.* New York: Bowker.

————. 1984b. "Patterns and Costs of Crime." *Library Trends* 33, no. 1: 69–76.

National Task Force on Emergency Response: Safeguarding Our Cultural Heritage. 1997. *Emergency Response and Salvage Wheel.* Available through the National Task Force on Emergency Response, 3299 K Street, N.W., Suite 602, Washington, D.C. 20003.

Paris, Janelle A. 1984. "Internal and External Responsibilities and Practices for Library Security." In *Security for Libraries: People, Buildings, Collections,* edited by Marvine Brand. Chicago: American Library Association.

Pettit, Katherine D. 1981. "Emergencies and Problems: A Procedures Manual for Trinity University Library." San Antonio, Tex.: Trinity University Library. ED214527.

Shaughnessy, Thomas W. 1984. "Security: Past, Present, and Future." In *Security for Libraries: People, Buildings, Collections,* edited by Marvine Brand. Chicago: American Library Association.

2 SECURITY OF THE GENERAL COLLECTION

PROBLEMS

Security issues have appeared at the forefront of library literature for many reasons. Recent reports of violence and aggression against library staff and users have raised awareness of the seriousness of the problem of security in libraries. Reported acts of violence include incidents in public, academic, urban, and rural libraries. (Shuman, 1996; 1997) Some factors contributing to the problem of security in libraries include an attitude of entitlement, the expectation of immediate gratification, financial concerns, ease of access, and the "Kenny" factor.

ATTITUDE OF ENTITLEMENT

Reported incidences of theft and mutilation continue to increase. Twenty-five years ago the reasons cited, in now-classic works, ranged from lack of money for photocopying to failure to remember the library card. (Hendrick and Murfin, 1974; Gouke and Murfin, 1980; Varner, 1983; Watstein, 1983; Lincoln, 1984; Brand, 1984; Pedersen, 1990) These reasons still apply. However, in addition, today we read stories like the one about a woman at Ohio University who ripped recipes and advertisements from *Gourmet Magazine* simply because she was bored and remembered liking carrot cake. Not only was she fully aware of what she was doing, she did not see her behavior as a problem. In fact, she was incensed at the library's reaction to her behavior. She then used her position as a student editor to write a very "in-your-face" editorial about the librarians who discovered her acts of vandalism and then reprimanded her for them. (Rovito, 1994) According to Chadbourne (1994: 23), young people today present an apathetic tolerance of criminal behavior.

EXPECTATION OF IMMEDIATE GRATIFICATION

Another factor contributing to the increase in theft and mutilation from the general collection is the societal norm of the day–NOW! In our culture there is the expectation that everything should be available instantly. This need for immediate gratification spills over into a need for information. Everyone is pressed and everyone needed it "yesterday." Multitasking, a computer word accepted in the broader culture, defines the information seeker of today. User stresses are unimaginable. In high schools, colleges, and universities, library users may be working full-time, have families, and attend school. Deadlines for work, for school, and for family members capture the attention of the users. Library hours are inadequate to meet the need for information that is delivered "just in time." Sometimes library materials are mistakenly grabbed when the frazzled user is packing up personal belongings and rushing off to make the next deadline. In special libraries, the organizations they support also require the information be delivered quickly and accurately.

FINANCIAL CONCERNS

Monetary concerns affect both library users and libraries. For example, from the user's point of view, the cost of books, particularly textbooks, is staggering. Many libraries add processing fees to bills for books—making theft an attractive option. The idea of stealing a book may be more attractive as the purchase price of the item increases. In public libraries, users may believe that the books, purchased from tax dollars, are theirs. Competition with bookstores, especially the large chains, may present a new twist to library security. At least superficially, bookstores seem able to give services quickly and with greater ambiance than public library branches. (Coffman, 1998) Often these large chain stores offer more comprehensive hours of operation than libraries are able to offer. Customers know that if they inadvertently damage an item or if they discover their need is greater than originally thought, they can easily purchase the item.

From the library's perspective, the budget is the biggest concern. Static budgets exacerbate the problems of theft and mutilation of the general collection. These budgets leave little money available for the purchase of replacements. If a library is to have a viable acquisitions program, the purchase of replacements will be low on the list of priorities. Due to inflation, the purchase power of replacement dollars is diminished. Compounding the problem of diminished capacity for replacements is the current speed with which items go out of print—making it impossible to buy replacements even if money is available.

EASE OF ACCESS

A tension exists today between the right of free access to information and the need to preserve information. Yet, St. Lifer (1994: 36) notes "by securing materials, . . . they *are* preserving access. After all, while the book or manuscript may be more difficult to get to, at least it's on the shelf in one piece." Closed stacks used to be the vogue. Then open stacks became the norm. Now libraries are struggling with the ideas of access management, restricted access, closed stacks, and adjusted service hours. The surge in digitized information creates opportunities to rethink the idea of physical access. It also creates new concerns for security—security of information and equipment. While librarians are trying to make information more available, they are also trying to devise ways to protect the collections and the people who use and work with them. This situation creates stresses for library staff who sometimes feel at cross-purposes with themselves.

"KENNY" FACTOR

Kenny is a cartoon character on the popular television show *South Park*. At the end of each episode, Kenny dies. It is a joke. In each subsequent episode, Kenny reappears. There is no explanation given for how the viewer could have misunderstood Kenny's prior death; the story just continues. Everyone knows he will be back next time. The only unknown is the newest creative and ghastly manner of his death. Students of popular culture say the "Kenny" factor describes an attitude alternatively of "So what?" and of "Who cares?" It is only a short step from those ideas to "It is only a book, how hard could it be to get another?" Kenny dies; he'll be back.

DEFINITIONS

Before an appropriate plan for securing the general collection can be designed, some key words need to be defined. For example, what is the definition of an "overdue" item? A "missing" item? What is the relationship between the two? What is "theft by conversion" and how does it relate to the security plan? Is the security plan going to address overdue items or just items that are missing in inventory? What is "mutilation"? How is it assessed? What is "theft"? Is there evidence of employee theft? How might these be related? A shared understanding of an operational definition of each of these words is necessary—regardless of the definition selected—in order to create a complete awareness of the scope of security of the general collection for each library.

OVERDUE, MISSING, LOST, OR STOLEN?

For purposes of security, most libraries treat overdue, missing, lost, and stolen items as four unique constructs.

"Overdues" are those items for which the circulation system has a valid location. Usually that location is a borrower. Although the item may be past its due date, it is not considered to be a violation of security because its location is recorded. Overdue notices and bills may have to be sent, but the location is known. Academic and school libraries usually have more leverage than public libraries to encourage the return of items. For example, grades may be withheld or registration may be blocked. Public libraries and some academic libraries may block future borrowing until the items are returned and appropriate fees are paid. Some library systems use collection agencies to help retrieve items. Some use amnesty days or grace periods to encourage returns without a penalty. Regardless, most libraries do not consider routine overdue items to be a part of the security problem and do not include them in an overall security plan. It is believed that overdue items are taken care of in a routine way.

After an item has languished for a long time in an overdue status, some libraries may use the legal avenue of "theft by conversion" to retrieve items. (That is, after a long time the library assumes the borrower has stolen the book by converting it to a personal collection.) However, the number of libraries doing that is limited. Libraries deciding to use this legal avenue should include mention of it in their overall security plan.

"Missing" items are usually those items that cannot be found either on the shelf or as charged to a borrower or location. Users identify most missing items as they look for titles they find in the catalog. They report the items as missing from the shelf and usually the circulation department looks for them. Members of library departments may also notice items missing as they go about their work. Also, items may be noted as missing in an inventory. While items that are missing very well may be the result of theft, they are also equally likely to have been misshelved. They could also have been hidden by someone who has no library card, be in use in the building, or be on a staff member's desk. Libraries should decide how they plan to account for these items in their security plan.

After a time, items that have not been found are considered "lost." Lost items may also include items formerly charged to patrons who subsequently paid for them because they admitted the item was lost while in their possession. Lost items may also be ones for which an extensive, but unsuccessful, search has been made over a period of months. Lost items would include items discovered to be missing in an inventory. Items missing and not found after an extensive period of searching may again very well be the by-product of a successful theft. However, while that cannot be known, for purposes of the overall security plan, lost items should be treated in the same way as missing items.

How then is "stolen" defined? Recognizing a stolen book is impossible. An item cannot be termed stolen unless there is hard evidence to support the idea that it is stolen. Such evidence would include witnessing the act of stealing. Employees may assume materials are stolen because they are missing, but in the legal sense, the items are just missing.

MUTILATION

"Mutilation" is a different story. Mutilation is the result of an act. As such, unless the culprit is actually seen in the act of mutilating the item, the book is just another damaged book. Some institutional security plans include examples of outcomes in cases where people have been observed in the act of mutilating library materials. However, mutilation is a difficult charge to prove unless the person who saw the act of mutilation is willing to testify or otherwise state that fact publicly.

What is easier to prove is the *result* of the act of mutilation. For purposes of the security plan, defining mutilation as the "observable result of activity" is useful. For example, making a charge against a user for exiting a security system with materials that show evidence of recent mutilation is easier than trying to prove that the person actually mutilated the item. Ohio State University defines mutilation as "damage, defacement, or destruction of library materials. . . . " (Association of Research Libraries, 1989: 53) Examples of evidence of recent mutilation may include:

- A missing call number label
- A missing bookplate
- A missing pocket
- A missing bar code label
- A sliced spine (possibly to reveal the presence of a metal target)
- A missing date due slip
- Pages from a periodical

THEFT

"Theft" is a legal term with many meanings that the courts and their jurisdictions control. "Theft by conversion" (converting library materials to ones' own property) is an example of theft. Most librarians think of theft as the act of stealing something from the library. However, how can the patron's intent be determined? If a patron says that he or she forgot to check out the material, is it still theft? If the library intends to prosecute or press any charges, there must be a foolproof system for determining if the intent was theft. At Georgia State University (GSU) in Atlanta, where users may be arrested, "theft by taking" is the legal charge frequently made when someone exits the security system with mutilated materials. GSU believes they cannot prove mutilation, but the fact that the item is mutilated provides probable cause to believe the person was attempting to steal the item. GSU will not arrest someone caught in the security system unless the item is mutilated in some way.

EMPLOYEE THEFT

Many security experts argue that employee theft is also a big problem. (Layne, 1994) Employees, they say, have access to library items before they are accessioned, entered into the system, and processed. Some consultants emphasize intensive preemployment screening and background checks to reduce the risk of employee theft. Others recommended key control, limited access to processing areas of the library, and prohibiting staff to work in the library during normally closed hours as ways of controlling employee theft. With the increase of integrated online library systems that track an item from the point of order to final shelving, the risk of theft from the processing stream is minimized. However, with distributed access to the circulation system, items may be charged and discharged from a person's record, or removed from the library in a variety of other ways. Restricting the points where items are charged, requiring borrower cards for all transactions, enforcing building closing times for all employees, and requiring everyone to exit from a controlled exit point should discourage employee theft. One large academic library even ceased allowing custodial services to work in the building when it is closed.

LOSS AND MUTILATION RATES

The security audit, described in Chapter 1, will provide a picture of the library's own vulnerabilities. Next, the library must obtain an understanding of its current loss and mutilation rates. Approaches to determining the loss and mutilation rates range from the simplistic—comparing the actual number of items reported missing or mutilated, or comparing the number of replacements ordered each year—to the mathematical. Three mathematical and statistically valid approaches are frequently used to obtain the loss and mutilation rates. These are an inventory, a census, and statistical sampling.

INVENTORY

An inventory is a systematic tracking of each volume a library's record shows it owns. It supplies author, title, and call number information for every missing or mutilated item. During an inventory, misshelved, mislabeled, and mutilated items may be found. Many traces are initiated, many orders for replacements may be made, many repairs are performed, and collection evaluation opportunities abound. Generally, a small library can do an annual inventory and compare from year to year the number of items missing or mutilated. This process provides the most accurate information on the loss and mutilation rates as well as specifics about what is lost or mutilated. It is extremely difficult, however, for a large library to complete a full inventory. Large academic and public libraries would find it very costly and disruptive to do this while remaining open to the public. School libraries are better able to execute such a project at the end of each school year when students are gone.

CENSUS

A census is another strategy used to learn loss and mutilation rates. A census targets specific areas and counts the number of volumes available and/or the number of mutilated items observed. To obtain the loss rate, this number plus the number of items with known locations (charged on the circulation system, for example) can be compared against the known total from the catalog record. The result is a number representing the gross number of items missing in specific segments of the collection. For a mutilation rate, the number of items needing repairs in one area can be compared to that number from the previous year in the same area. The advantages of a census over an inventory are that attention is focused in a specific area, it is less costly, it takes less time than an inventory, and it can be completed while the library is open. The main disadvantage of a census is that the results cannot be applied to the larger collection. Using a census to identify mutilated items presents the challenge of distinguishing between items mutilated and items showing signs of normal wear and tear.

STATISTICAL SAMPLING

Sampling is a statistically sound way of predicting the rate of missing or mutilated items for the entire collection. In a sample designed to measure loss, every nth item in the record is compared to the official record, the shelf, and the circulation file. In a sample designed to measure mutilation, every nth item is evaluated and rated. Statistical sampling may be used in an inventory of the entire collection or of a specific piece of the collection. Though still labor-intensive and time-consuming, statistical sampling is useful in a large collection because the results can be projected to the entire collection.

COST OF THE LOSSES

After the loss and mutilation rates are determined, the cost of these losses to the library can be computed. There are a variety of ways to calculate this cost. Several publications record the overall average cost of an item, the average cost of an item in specific subject areas, and/or the average cost of an item in specific Library of Congress classifications. For example, *Bowker Annual Library and Book Trade Almanac* (New York: R. R. Bowker) is a popular assessment tool. Vendors provide guides to their publishing output, including average prices. Also, Gale publishes the *Bookman's Price Index. American Book Prices Current* is published by Bancroft-Parkman. Multiplying average costs by the total number of missing or mutilated items yields the figure for an estimated cost of the loss. By completing this process annually, figures can be compared, for example, before and after implementing changes in policy or procedure.

Note, however, that this figure for an estimated loss only accounts for the actual cost of the specific items. To obtain a realistic estimate of the actual cost to the library, the rate also would have to be inflated to include an estimate of "the value-added costs library materials must command." (Stack, 1998: 27) That is, direct cataloging and computer costs to remove the items from the collection and to add replacements must be included. In addition, an estimate for the cost of staff time needed for a variety of responsibilities related to repair or replacement must be presented. Expenditures for professional expertise and staff time include making collection evaluation decisions about replacement, repair, or withdrawal; adjusting the records; reordering appropriate missing or damaged items; and processing the new items when they are received.

Stack urges that the cost for the incalculables—such as time spent by patrons and staff searching for missing items and the impact on the service ethos when items are missing—must also be incorporated. He further urges libraries to consider the retail arena when making "return-on-investment" decisions. In retailing, all costs are considered, including those for replacement and theft. (Stack, 1998: 26–27)

DEVELOPING A PROPOSAL

Once the rates of loss and mutilation are identified and the estimated cost to the library is determined, a proposal for securing the general collection must be developed. This proposal should include:

- An overall ideal recommendation for collection security
- The projected cost of implementation
- A plan for phasing in the initiatives over several years
- A prioritized list of the elements

Such a security proposal allows the governing bodies to see a range of excellent suggestions for securing the general collection and permits them to select important elements while considering the ranked needs identified by the library.

There are many places to find sample proposals, including in "SPEC kits," available through the Association of Research Libraries, Office of Management Services, Systems and Procedures Exchange Center. These publications provide a variety of excellent examples arranged by topic. For example, SPEC kit Number 100 deals with collection security in ARL libraries; SPEC kit Number 150 is about building security and safety. While some information in the SPEC kits might be dated for a reporting institution, the kits are valuable resources for clever ideas.

Besides including the results of the environmental audit, the loss and mutilation rates, and the projected cost to the library, a security proposal for the general collection should include consideration of administrative and social issues. For example, administrative support, available personnel, internal policies, relevant local ordinances and laws, funding, and enforcement should be addressed.

ADMINISTRATIVE SUPPORT

What level of corrective or punitive action will be supported by the administration, the board, or the community? The answer to this question is critical to developing suggestions for securing the general collection. A range of probable outcomes will need to be developed and presented. Probable outcomes could include:

- Fines
- Fees
- Warnings
- Counseling
- Mediation
- Community service
- Referrals
- Arrest
- Adjudication

Support for whatever plan is adopted must be obtained at the beginning of the project. For example, if the library board supports a predetermined solution for a security problem, a security proposal will probably not be requested. Rather, it would be politically best to implement the board's idea early in the planning process. However, securing permission to complete a full security proposal is important to permit the library and its board to explore all possibilities. In an open environment or once permission has been secured, points at which administrators need to be involved in the daily operation of the plan should be clear. Decisions regarding purchases, contracts, and maintenance agreements will have to be made at the highest level.

One common occurrence is the funding of an electronic book-theft-detection system with little planning. When this is done, the assumption is it will automatically enhance security. Electronic book-theft-detection systems do enhance some elements of security to the general collection, of course. However, when the idea to purchase such a system is made before the completion of a security proposal, a major planning element is missed. That is, what is the answer to the following question: "What are you going to do when the alarm sounds?" (Cravey, Robison, and Russell, 1984: 317; Luurtsema, 1997) A comprehensive security plan would include an answer to that question as an aspect of administrative support.

AVAILABLE PERSONNEL

Issues of personnel are critical to make the plan effective. Decisions to be made include those related to the employment levels of personnel needed for implementation, the source of and training of those employees, and authority. If current employees are to be diverted from other jobs to support the security plan, these employees need to be identified and planned for early in the implementation process. Additionally, other employees might be needed. If other administrative units, such as the local police force, could supply some of these needs, that would be an asset to the library. Some public libraries have established a beat office right in the library. Often such offices are used as sites where officers can prepare routine paperwork. In these instances, police officers have a comfortable place of their own to use whenever necessary and the library benefits from an increased police presence.

Once the final plan is implemented, if it includes confronting users, relevant local ordinances and laws will need to be consulted to decide the appropriate level of employee to handle such responsibilities. (Bielefield and Cheeseman, 1995) Regardless of who is chosen to implement the plan, thorough initial and ongoing training are essential and should be included as an integral part of the plan.

INTERNAL POLICIES

When the selected solution involves humans, policies regarding attire, decorum, and vocabulary must be decided. If building patrols are designed to stop acts of mutilating library materials, it will be important to know if they are also to stop other problems, such as smoking or consuming food. An outcome that involves arresting violators will require a decision on how to handle such issues as what to do when an employee is called to court on a regular day off. Further, who will represent the staff member if a jury trial is requested? Who will be authorized to call for a criminal trespass warning for people accused of mutilating library materials? Who will be eligible to sign legal forms as a library official? If machines are to be used for the plan, issues such as the following must be addressed:

- Definition of a "false alarm"
- Definitions and examples supporting the final outcomes (definition of "mutilation" if an arrest is to be made for mutilation, for example)
- Proper responses for possible machine malfunctions

Again, ongoing training is critical to the success of the plan.

RELEVANT LOCAL ORDINANCES AND LAWS

Depending on the solutions selected, local ordinances and laws must be considered. While laws vary by jurisdiction, several discussions of possibilities are available (Robison, Marshall, and Cravey, 1992: 164–167). For example, some jurisdictions will allow policies to vary by type of library user. Colleges may prefer to handle security matters regarding their own students differently from the way they handle community users. In these cases, students may be referred to a dean or to the student judicial system while non-college personnel may be arrested and referred to the court system. Some legal jurisdictions may accept this arrangement and others may not.

Each institution must define terms related to theft and mutilation. These definitions should include an explanation of who will make the assessments and what criteria they will use. A comprehensive plan will include strategies for persons who claim the incident is a mistake or a library error. Planners must address age, racial, socioeconomic, cultural, and gender differences. Regardless of the outcome selected, offenders will be well aware of these differences and will notice (and report) differential treatment.

If a library intends to warn a violator on a first offense but take action on the second offense, it will need to develop a "tracking" system to know the history of the violator. Warnings and trespassing warnings are examples of preliminary warnings. If the legal Criminal Trespass Warning system is used for the first offense, subsequent offenses could result in an arrest for trespassing. Criminal trespassing following such a formal warning is an easy offense to prove in court. Plans for tracking initial and subsequent offenses need to be addressed in the security proposal.

All policies must be in writing. In addition, signs may need to be posted alerting library users to library policy. Signs citing the state code or the institution's honor codes may be posted so users can have a clear understanding of the library's intent. Wording for such signs may require legal assistance.

FUNDING

Setting up a viable system for securing the general collection could be very expensive, perhaps costing much more than what is available. Planners should think of the proposal in stages. A phased implementation plan, or a plan that breaks the proposal into categories of "no cost," "low cost," "medium cost," and "expensive," will usually be appreciated by the fiscal officer. The proposal should include possible sources of extramural funding. Grants, gifts from Friends groups, and gifts from the senior class, could be solicited in the proposal-writing stage. If the plan is to address a problem situation that is receiving publicity, a bond referendum may be an appropriate way to obtain the necessary funding. Often costs can be shared among agencies. For example, the library and the police may be able to share the cost of increased library security.

ENFORCEMENT

A decision on the employment level of personnel who enforce the decisions is critical. Laws regarding the level of employees used, the powers they have, and the words they may use may vary by jurisdiction. For example, a library official may be able to say "May I *check* your bag?" but may not be able to say "May I *search* your bag?" In most circumstances, "search" is a legal term. A search cannot be undertaken without a properly executed search warrant. In these cases, however, it may be appropriate to ask permission to "check" a person's belongings. Once such permission is given, a thorough check through the belongings would be appropriate. The powers of searching and arresting are spelled out carefully in local codes.

It is imperative to be aware of the legal powers that are possible for the type of person hired to do the job and then to adhere to them. For example, a security guard may have the power to detain but not to arrest. A student employee may be able to detain and not question. The definition of these legal powers may vary by state. However, usually only a police officer may arrest.

TYPES OF SOLUTIONS

There are no generic "best scenario" solutions available for securing the library's general collection. One library's solution will not necessarily work for another. It is useful, though, to review others' solutions prior to writing a formal proposal. There are three steps to incorporate this type of review into the proposal-writing stage. First, a look at what others are doing could result in identifying solutions that are directly transferable from one institution to another. Second, other solutions that could not be adopted directly might be appropriately adapted for use by other libraries. Third, viewing others' solutions should create an environment where brainstorming leads to the revelation of other innovative ideas.

Several types of security solutions might be chosen to help protect the general collection. These may be classed as low-intensity, medium-intensity, and high-intensity solutions. They can be used alone or in concert.

LOW-INTENSITY SOLUTIONS

Low-intensity solutions are noninvasive. Several classic and innovative low-intensity solutions are described below.

Adjusted Hours

Service hours may need to be reduced in order to distribute staff over a smaller range of hours in a broader range of locations. It may be determined that certain hours of the day represent the greatest number of occurrences of damage to the general collection; the library may elect to close during those hours. Some consultants also believe it is important to restrict staff attendance only to open hours.

Amnesty Days

An old strategy, amnesty days were designed to get missing items back into the library with no penalty to the person returning the item. While these days are now designed to have a fine-free period for book returns, they could also bring long-overdue, missing, and mutilated items back to the library. A classic concern with the idea of amnesty days is that users may hold on to all material until such days.

Checkroom

A central checkroom, where personal items are given over to an attendant who offers a receipt or claim check, is another approach. This option might work in a library with light traffic but could also cause jams at the entrance as well as at the exit. Additionally, by the time patrons entered the main part of the library they could already be angry about the delay at the door. The library would also probably have some liability if users claimed items were missing from their personal belongings after they were left in the checkroom.

Closed Stacks

For the general collection, these options are vestigial reminders of bygone days. To close the stacks now seems antithetical to the mission of modern libraries. In fact, so foreign is this concept that in libraries that still have closed stacks they are not thought of as an extension of the general collection. The biggest concerns with closed stacks—whether they exist now or are being considered as a solution to theft from the general collection—are being able to justify the area and being able to afford the continuing costs associated with item retrieval. Modern advocates of closed stacks suggest that since the automated catalogs offer increasingly sophisticated search strategies, there is no need to offer browsing in the stack areas.

Digitizing

The provision of inexpensive copies of popular items in digitized format could help stop theft of the print copies. Issues to be resolved include copyright, staff time, users to be targeted, and format of the information (download to disk but not print, for example).

Duplicates

Another popular idea is that popular titles are unlikely to be stolen if multiple copies are available. This might be a good solution in public libraries or for popular rental collections; however, for academic libraries it is difficult to justify these additional copies.

Lobby Reconfiguration

Various designs of the lobby area of the library may be considered to enhance security or to enhance the appearance of security. Holt (1979: 1–20) describes seven traditional ways the entrance/exit/circulation desk area can be designed to enhance security. His models range from open and flowing to a series of aisles and walkways. In one model, he places activities supporting entrance (book return, fine payment, and registration) at the entrance and activities supporting exit (checking out books) at the exit. This arrangement essentially created two service desks and projected a significantly enhanced appearance of security as well as actually enhancing security to the collection. It also may have had an impact on staffing either by requiring additional staff at the second service point or by splitting existing staff between the two service points.

Lockers

Lockers can be made available for users while they are in the library. Similar to those in airports, lockers may solve the problem of clutter or hiding places around the library. Lockers could be rented for a fee or keys could be checked out as a short-term loan, like books. If lockers are available, the library should plan for reports of thefts from the lockers, responsibility for protecting the lockers, and liability if someone claims something was stolen from rented lockers. Lockers also usually require maintenance, such as for broken locks, forgotten keys, and checks to be sure library materials are not being hidden in them as a way to avoid the circulation process.

Photocopy Services

The idea that good quality and inexpensive photocopy services will reduce the theft from the general collection seems to be a "given" in library circles. The questions, though, of *how* inexpensive and *how* good the service must be seem to be unanswerable. Inexpensive service and quality print will reduce some of the theft and mutilation, but a lot of people will steal for other reasons. In today's library market, anything that requires a user to wait even as little as three minutes seems to be reason to take what is needed. If the library were to provide an inexpensive photocopying service, the cost to various constituents would need to be determined. For example, in an academic library, would that institution's students be the only users qualified for inexpensive copying? What about in public libraries? Would there be a cost recovery factor or a more expensive copying option for non-students or non-residents?

Property Marking

One of the easiest things a library can do is to have an all-out program of property marking. The more markings in a book, the harder it is to remove the evidence that the item belongs to the library. For example, bar codes, book pockets, date due slips, bookplates, and call number labels all identify the item as a library book. So, too, do call numbers written inside the item and accession numbers stamped somewhere in the item. Another useful marking is to have the library name stamped on all three of the edges of the book. When the library and the institution names are stamped in a bold color along the edges of a book, staff searching for the cause of a security alarm can quickly spot a mutilated book in a backpack. Stamping edges can be done at service desks, on a time available basis, as books are checked in.

Reserves

The reserves system seems to have evolved as a way of placing certain heavily used items in protective custody while permitting short-term borrowing. This strategy is so institutionalized now that few people think of it as a solution to theft. Moving to electronic reserves will address some of the concerns of placing general collection items in closed stacks while creating an array of additional quandaries. For example, restricting access to course reserves only to students enrolled in the class, digitizing copyrighted items, and digitizing noncopyrighted information (like student papers)—which might also be a violation of privacy laws—all have to be addressed.

Restricted Access

Unlike closed stacks, restricted access provides access to the general collection to sets of predetermined clientele who present proper identification or authorization. For example, unrestricted access could be provided to a government documents depository collection, while access to the rest of the general collection could be denied to people without specific authorizations. Such access could be controlled by cards or by monitors.

Staff Badges

Badges can be used to identify people who should be in certain areas performing certain tasks. For example, someone from a processing unit might be pulling periodicals from the shelf and marking them in some way. If users saw that activity they might think the person was mutilating an item rather than preparing it for binding. These badges have many uses beyond protecting the general collection, but drawing attention to staffing levels is one of the more important uses. The greater the number of staff visible and identifiable out on the floors, the greater security to the collection will seem to be.

Storage Bins

Storage bins or storage shelves at the entrance represent another low-intensity solution. Users could be required to stow belongings at the door. This solution has a few drawbacks. Drawbacks include:

- The very likely problem of theft from the bins or shelves
- The issue of the library's liability in such theft
- Delays at the entrance as users hunt for space
- Delays at the exit as users try to retrieve their personal belongings

Turnstiles

Another older solution, turnstiles give the appearance of increased security and attention to the materials in the library. Often coupled with a guard of some sort, turnstiles send the message that the library is concerned about the collection.

MEDIUM-INTENSITY SOLUTIONS

Following are solutions that have a moderate amount of indirect personal invasion. Often they involve specialized staff. Whenever staff, specialized or regular, are used for security to the general collection, the library should have a clear understanding of the mission, responsibilities, duties, interactions, and qualifications required to do the job, prior to engaging in this methodology. (Walsh and Healy, 1979)

Additional Staff

An increase in staff is an approach tried as a medium-intensity means of providing security to the general collection. The sheer increase in numbers is probably not very effective, however, unless the additional staff members are strategically placed. For example, increasing staff on each floor of a building is probably useful even if the employees are in an office area behind a closed door. Patrons would think they could go to that office if they saw or experienced a problem. Holt (1979: 18) suggests that additional staff is a useful option only if service desks are involved and if they are aligned so as to provide a clear view of the stacks areas. Mirrors could also assist staff in monitoring the stacks.

Contract Security

Professional security guards, contracted from local agencies, may present advantages not possible with internal solutions. For example, guards may be older adults and therefore may command more respect or courtesy than internal employees. Licensing requirements for contract security vary by state—in some states they do not have to be licensed. It is important to know what the hiring agency's requirements are for contracted security. If walking through the building is one responsibility, the job can be very physical. Security personnel could be at risk in isolated areas of the building. If the job involves sitting, it could be boring or unrewarding. Finally, clear policies as to what the contracted security personnel should do or say if they find someone committing a violation must be developed.

Door Guards

There are several ways to use door guards to enhance security to the general collection. Early door guards actually inspected book bags and briefcases, looking through them for improperly charged library materials. Pass-around security systems require a human situated at the exit to receive the items and pass them around the sensors. Door guards may also be used in conjunction with the electronic theft detection system in some instances. In cases where the electronic exit is not contiguous to a public service desk, door guards may sit at the exit assisting people whose belongings have set off the alarm. In those cases, guards may be able to monitor the entrance for food and drink, and answer routine directional questions. One glaring problem with door guards is boredom. To be effective, door guards cannot study or read. But when there is little traffic in the library, door guards can get slack and give a bad first impression of the library.

Electronic Book-Theft-Detection Systems

These systems are common security solutions in modern society. They may be classed as electromagnetic, radio frequency, acousta-magnetic, and microwave. These systems offer approximately 80–85 percent reduction in losses. The electromagnetic and radio frequency systems, such as those found in airports and drug stores, are also the most appropriate for libraries. Decisions to make regarding the purchase of electronic theft-detection systems are aided by numerous catalogs and checklists prepared by vendors and outside consultants. Lists and evaluations of vendors for a variety of electronic theft-detection systems may be found in *Library Technology Reports*, published by the American Library Association; *The Librarian's Yellow Pages*, published by Garance; and others.

All electronic theft-detection systems require several components. First, a detection device is inserted into each item to be protected. These devices are variously called targets, tags, beepers, strips, and other names. They are specific to the type of system selected and must be purchased in conjunction with that system. Second, electronic sensor panels, or the alarm annunciation center, installed at exits are designed to limit egress and to interrogate each exit attempt for the presence of the detection device. The third component is an accessory that will remove or reinstate the "activity" of the detection device—either a magnet system or a "detuning" device. In both types of systems, an alarm sounds if the sensor detects items that have not been properly treated for the exit. A properly charged-out item has the "charge" removed and the user is free to exit the library as long as the alarm does not sound. (Stack, 1998: 28–33) Electronic book-theft-detection systems are expensive solutions to the problem of securing the general collection. The initial investment can be quite large. Continuing costs of purchasing and inserting the detection devices, updating maintenance agreements, and monitoring costs must also be included when weighing this option.

How the exit will be monitored—so that if the sensor alarm sounds, a user will know to come back to be checked—is another important concern with electronic theft-detection systems. In the ideal sense, if the exit is near a service desk, usually the circulation desk, then existing staff can attend to the alarms as a part of their normal workday. There should be no need for additional staff.

Emergency Telephones

Another solution is the installation of police emergency telephones in various locations. These telephones can be set to alarm at the police headquarters when the handset is removed from its cradle. A floor location would be associated with that telephone, so a police response would be assured if someone experienced difficulty on an upper floor or in a remote area. The person would not even have to speak into the telephone for the emergency response to be supplied. This could be a very popular solution for extramural funding.

In-House Monitors

In-house human monitors can be assigned to patrol the building to be on the lookout for mutilation. Monitors can be students and they also can look out for other infractions. For example, they may be able to enforce the food, drink, and smoking policy of the building. Sometimes in-house monitors are easy targets for harassment and they are thus difficult to retain. The effectiveness of a monitor—particularly a student—is questionable. Abusers would clearly wait until the monitor had passed before committing an act of vandalism. Some of the same concerns for the duties and qualifications of contract security also apply to monitors.

Staff Training

It is important that staff be prepared for issues related to security of the general collection. As they move about the building they are the extra eyes and ears necessary to spot unusual activity. If they are to accost users in any way, staff will need intensive training in the legally correct way to do so. Role-playing and a strong supervisory presence early in the training are essential to combat the normal fear that most people have when confronting others. Security experts can be brought in, police have special community outreach units that offer training, and experienced staff can mentor new staff.

HIGH-INTENSITY SOLUTIONS

Many libraries—especially large public libraries—use contracted security, police presence, or metered police patrols. These solutions work in a variety of ways to stem all types of crime in the library. They are often used in conjunction with more intense systems. Several high-intensity systems are discussed below.

Access Management Systems

Access management systems are increasing in popularity. Sign-in systems at the front door, the surrendering of some important form of identification, being photographed, and closed-circuit television are all being used to help manage the entrance to the building. Some of these techniques have been in use in special collections and archives for a long time and have proven successful. Concerns include balancing the public's right to access and the library's right to maintain a collection, as well as continuing costs, and public relations.

Closed-Circuit Television (CCTV)

In this system the general collection may be protected from those users so intent on theft that they ignore the security system by tossing items from windows, use fire exits, or mutilate items in secure remote places within the building. Concerns for CCTV include issues of privacy and continuing costs for monitoring. If videotaping is used, storage requirements must also be considered.

Radio-Frequency Identification (RF-ID)

RF-ID systems are invisible bar codes, proximity cards, cash cards, debit cards, and many other applications rolled into one computer chip. These devices can track all activities in the stacks and at the point of self-charging. If a patron carrying an RF-ID card exited the building without checking out books and then ignored the gate alarm and continued through the exit, the RF-ID would provide information about the patron and all the books involved. (Stack, 1998: 35–37) The initial cost would be great, especially since all patrons would have to have such a card and all items would need to have the chip inserted. However, this is another application where several offices could share the cost.

Robotics

Right now the use of robotics in securing the general collection is not seriously reported. However, there are tongue-in-cheek fantasy systems of behavioral modification, such as the one dubbed P.E.S.T., designed to encourage the cessation of various types of inappropriate behavior in libraries. With the Problem Eradicator Service Technology system, arms are suspended unobtrusively from tracks in the ceiling. Computers activate the arms when they spot inappropriate behavior—mutilation, for example. A series of progressively threatening activities occur if the patron ignores the warnings of the system.

The ultimate outcome is the patron's removal from the building via robotic arm! (Horak, 1997)

SUMMARY

Planning for and executing a security plan for the general collection are daunting events. A committee of involved staff members can be created to look at the areas named above and to design the initial proposal. This process will take many hours of work but it will be well worth it in the end. Using a committee to do the initial plan accommodates the expertise of the front-line employees while fostering an environment conducive to staff buy-in to the finished product.

It is interesting to note that the literature of security in libraries and other places frequently refers to the "appearance" of security. For example, door guards, mirrors, staff badges, and registration all are designed to improve the appearance of diligent attention to security. These elements may actually improve the sense that the building is being carefully monitored, but they really do not do much to improve the condition of the general collection. Often a lot of mileage can be gained from improving the appearance!

To summarize, the security of the general collection depends on a detailed security proposal and subsequent plan. The final proposal should include the following items:

- Reference to the security audit, highlighting current vulnerabilities
- Reference to the documented loss and mutilation rates of the organization and the concomitant costs
- Reference to relevant administrative and social issues
- Overall recommendation
- Projected cost of implementation
- Prioritized list of elements
- Plan for phasing in the elements over several years, including sources of extramural funding
- Plan for what to do when someone is caught by the system
- Plan for initial and ongoing training

REFERENCES

Association of Research Libraries—Office of Management Services—The Systems and Procedures Exchange Center. 1984. *#100, Collection Security in ARL Libraries.* Washington, D.C.: Association of Research Libraries, Office of Management Studies.

———. 1989. *#150, Building Security and Personal Safety.* Washington, D.C.: Association of Research Libraries, Office of Management Studies.

Bielefield, Arlene, and Lawrence Cheeseman. 1995. *Library Patrons and the Law.* New York: Neal-Schuman.

Brand, Marvine, ed. 1984. *Security for Libraries: People, Buildings, Collections.* Chicago: American Library Association.

Chadbourne, Robert. 1994. "Disorderly Conduct: Crime and Disruptive Behavior in the Library." *Wilson Library Bulletin* 68 (March): 23–25.

Coffman, Steve. 1998. "What If You Ran Your Library Like a Bookstore?" *American Libraries* 29, no. 3 (March): 40–42.

Cravey, Pamela J., Carolyn L. Robison, and Ralph E. Russell. 1984. "The Myth of Collection Security in Urban University Libraries." In *Proceedings of the ACRL Third National Conference, Seattle, April 4–7, 1984.* Chicago: American Library Association.

Gouke, Mary Noel, and Marjorie Murfin. 1980. "Periodical Mutilation: The Insidious Disease." *Library Journal* 105 (September 15): 1795–1797.

Hendrick, Clyde, and Marjorie Murfin. 1974. "Project Library Ripoff: A Study of Periodical Mutilation in a University Library." *College & Research Libraries* 35 (November): 402–404.

Holt, Raymond M. 1979. "Libraries." In *Handbook of Building Security Planning and Design,* edited by Peter S. Hopf. New York: McGraw-Hill.

Horak, Daniel. 1997. "P.E.S.T. (Problem Eradicator Service Technology): A High-Tech Solution to Library Vandalism and Crime." *Library & Archival Security* 14, no. 1: 75–80.

Layne, Stevan P. 1994. *The Official Library Security Manual.* Dillon, Co.: Layne Consultants International.

Lincoln, Alan Jay. 1984. *Crime in the Library: A Study of Patterns Impact, and Security.* New York: Bowker.

Luurtsema, David. 1997. "Dealing with Book Loss in an Academic Library." *Library & Archival Security* 14, no. 1: 21–27.

Pedersen, Terri L. 1990. "Theft and Mutilation of Library Materials." *College & Research Libraries* 51, no. 2 (March): 120–128.

Robison, Carolyn L., John D. Marshall, Jr., and Pamela J. Cravey. 1992. "Legal and Practical Aspects of Securing the General Collection in Academic Libraries." In *Academic Libraries in Urban and Metropolitan Areas: A Management Handbook,* edited by Gerard B. McCabe. New York: Greenwood Press.

Rovito, Lisa Marie. 1994. "Busted at the Library: I Tore Out a Page; They Tore Out My Heart, Fulfilling a Writer's Dream." *The Post* (Ohio University), 21 April. The article and reactions were posted on the CIRCPLUS listserv on 21 April 1994, by Margaret Robinson Arnold, Bindery Supervisor, Atkins Library, University of North Carolina, Charlotte. The subject line of the message was "Unmitigated Gall."

Shuman, Bruce A. 1996. "Designing Personal Safety into Library Buildings." *American Libraries* 27 (August): 37–39.

———. 1997. "The Devious, the Distraught and the Deranged: Designing and Applying Personal Safety into Library Protection." *Library & Archival Security* 14, no. 1: 53–73.

St. Lifer, Evan. 1994. "How Safe Are Our Libraries?" *Library Journal* (August): 35–39.

Stack, Michael J. 1998. "Library Theft Detection Systems: Future Trends and Present Strategies." *Library & Archival Security* 14, no. 2: 25–37.

Varner, Carroll. 1983. "Journal Mutilation in Academic Libraries." *Library & Archival Security* 5, no. 4: 19–27.

Walsh, Timothy J., and Richard J. Healy. 1979. "Security Personnel." In *Handbook of Building Security Planning and Design*, edited by Peter S. Hopf. New York: McGraw-Hill.

Watstein, Sarah Barbara. 1983. "Book Mutilation: An Unwelcome By-Product of Electronic Security Systems." *Library and Archival Security* 5, no. 1: 11–33.

3 SECURITY OF USERS AND EMPLOYEES

EXPECTATIONS OF A SAFE ENVIRONMENT

There are multiple ways to approach the security of library users and staff. In many cases the needs of both groups are similar. In other cases there are differences. However, both groups would agree that safety and security in and around the library is an important consideration. To that end, an American Library Association subcommittee has prepared guidelines for library security. Early in the document, the role of library administrators, vis-à-vis safety and security, is explained. The section of the draft detailing "Foreseeability of Loss" begins: "The Library Director . . . should be responsible for . . . anticipating, and taking measures to prevent predictable losses such as minor vandalism, injuries, theft of library materials or library user property. . . ." (American Library Association, 1999: 5) The document also outlines the responsibility of the director to collect and organize information related to such losses so that this information can be used to anticipate and prevent further losses. (American Library Association, 1999: 6) Users, staff, and administrators all have expectations for security and safety.

WHAT USERS EXPECT FROM STAFF

Users expect a clean and well-lighted facility where their reading and research needs are met comfortably and safely. They want to be able to roam the open-stack library without fear of physical attack, unwanted sexual attention, or distraction. They want to leave a coat or a book bag on a table "for just a minute" without fear that it will be stolen. Many want to tend to their needs and leave as quickly as possible. Others' goals are to remain in the library for an extended time using the Internet, researching family genealogy, reading reserves, or biding time between classes in a dry or warm spot. Users expect that staff have the means to make this possible. In fact, until recently, users did not think much about this sense of security. After all, it was a library! However unrealistic these expectations might seem to practicing librarians, crime reports and editorials related to criminal activities in libraries are full of tales supporting the idea that these are the users' expectations.

WHAT USERS AND STAFF EXPECT FROM EACH OTHER

All people expect and should demand to be treated with courtesy, respect, and civility. Library users expect safety and security to be dealt with unobtrusively by staff. Employees expect users to use "common sense" and to realize they are in a public place.

WHAT STAFF EXPECT FROM ADMINISTRATORS

Library employees expect a clear sense of direction and leadership from administrators. They, too, expect a clean and safe place in which to spend their working hours. The staff expects to be free from intruders in technical service spaces and free from verbal harassment and threat at public service points. Employees want to be able to use protective gloves, masks, and panic buttons when they think it is necessary. They want clear guidelines and procedures on how to handle threats, aberrant behavior, building emergencies, and the like. They want these guidelines to recognize the differences in the quantity and levels of staffing during weekday, weekend, and evening hours. They want to be able to pay well enough to attract qualified, personable, mature employees for public service and security functions—especially in the evenings and on weekends. ALA guidelines specify that the role of the library administration is in "safeguarding the physical protection of both library employees and library patrons" and in "ensuring that library employees are informed and instructed of their obligations in safety and security matters. . . ." (American Library Association, 1999: 5)

WHAT USERS, STAFF, AND ADMINISTRATORS EXPECT

All users, staff, and administrators expect clean and safe rest rooms with hot and cold water available from appropriate faucets, sanitized water fountains, and the freedom to walk appropriate corridors, aisles, and the perimeter of the building safely and without unwanted distraction of any type. They want to know that at some level of authority these things are being "handled" so they can do their job—be it work, study, pleasure, research, or catching a nap. Users especially want the issues of safety and security to be a given.

Building security and personal safety are the two aspects of a safe environment that both users and employees anticipate when they enter the library.

BUILDING SECURITY

Much of the literature on building security relates to fire, natural disasters, response procedures, and electronic book-theft-detection systems. While these issues are important concerns, they are outside the scope of this chapter. Additionally, building security encompasses much more than these few important elements. Global thinking is required in addressing building security.

Planning is the most critical aspect in the building security arena. If a new building is being planned it is easy to incorporate security right into the design. It is the job of the librarian to stress to the planners that building security is as important an issue as service. If, however, work on securing users and staff is being designed for an existing building, thoughts will have to be more creative.

ENVIRONMENTAL SCAN

An environmental scan is an excellent tool to help identify the variables to consider in building security. Such a scan will also help detail the specific vulnerabilities of each library. Each library has a unique personality, role, and set of characteristics. The environmental scan for each library should reflect the unique aspects of the library while addressing the importance of various risks related to security of that individual facility. Fennelly (1989: 37–46) provides many seemingly dated but still useful checklists that can be adapted to an environmental scan for a library. O'Block (1989: 21) refers to designs that result from an environmental scan as CPTED (Crime Prevention Through Environmental Design). Developing an environmental scan would be a good project for a task force consisting of library staff, users, administrators, and board members.

Just as each library is different, the design of each environmental scan and its results will be different. Among the variables libraries might want to consider in an environmental scan are:

- Local crime levels
- Actual risk versus the imagined risk
- Costs associated with increasing protection
- Resources available to devote to increased protection
- Stakeholders' viewpoints
- Realistic possibility of restricting access or egress

It is better, however, to let the task force identify things that need mentioning than to impose elements from the top or to glean them from a literature review.

Focus groups might be used in the design phase of the environmental scan. These groups could identify the critical areas of security needing attention. Such groups could also recognize the difficulties in providing adequate security.

Planners should also recognize ad hoc opportunities for input. For example, at one large urban university, a graduate student in the women's studies program claimed she was the recipient of repeated unwanted sexual attention in the library's stacks. By the time the police would arrive, the suspect had easily disappeared within the library's maze of floors. Exasperated, this woman mobilized the faculty and students in the women's studies program. Soon there were several protesters marching in front of the library, and signs and flyers were placed all over campus warning people about the lack of security in the library. Finally, a meeting was called of librarians, faculty, students, university lawyers, and campus police—including the police chief. There, the chief revealed her plan for increasing security for the library in the form of a security patrol. The library had tried to implement such a solution several years before but was thwarted by a lack of funds. The police chief's plan was funded by the police budget. This roving security patrol created a visible presence in the library. In addition, the existing patrol of plainclothes officers was increased. Incidents of problems in the stacks were virtually eliminated!

VULNERABILITIES IDENTIFIED

Vulnerabilities to consider in the environmental scan may include the perimeter of the building, lighting and alarm systems, parking lots, landscaping, windows, doors, keys, locks, rest room access, building design, building core, sight lines to the stacks, and hazards posed by eating, drinking, and smoking.

Perimeter of the Building

Frequent walks around the perimeter of the building will reveal vulnerabilities. Findings could include broken, unlatched, or open windows; unattended ladders near windows; books tossed out of windows; and locations for inappropriate or illegal activities. The perimeter check should include out-of-sight areas, such as attics, roofs, storage rooms, atria, and balconies. These areas should be routinely surveyed. Stairwells leading to rooftops are frequently places for illicit activity.

Lighting Systems

Lighting should be available throughout the library. Lights should be routinely checked and quickly replaced when bulbs are no longer working. The exterior of the building should be well lighted. All points of entry should be lighted even when the library is closed. Additional lighting should be available and used for stairs, access ramps, loading docks, or other access paths. External book drops should be well lighted.

Alarm Systems

Security alarms include electronic intrusion-detection systems and annunciation systems. Intrusion-detection systems should be installed on all doors. They should be operational at all times on all but the main entrances and exits. During closed times, they should be operational for all entrances and exits. Annunciation systems alert people to potentially dangerous situations. To that end, such building emergency alarms should be loud enough to be heard throughout the complex—including in rest rooms and in offices. These alarms should be supplemented with appropriate flashing devices for people with hearing impairments. Ideally, an alarm system would tie directly into that of a local police or fire system. Such a system would indicate the area where the alarm was first sounded. Evacuation procedures should be in place and should be known by staff. During some dangerous situations, such as bomb threats, the annunciation alarms often cannot be activated and the telephones cannot be used—either could trigger an explosion. Plans also need to be in place for evacuation due to bomb threats or other emergencies that preclude the use of the telephone. The use of motion detectors at closed hours should be considered—especially in large facilities with abundant hiding places. In some libraries, the use of a back-up generator in case of damage to the main power source is also critical.

Parking Lots

Parking lots should be well lighted and free of obstructions behind which someone could hide. Emergency phones should be available in each lot. A camera system, although expensive, would go a long way to enhancing security. Security guards, such as contracted security, could monitor the lots and front doors in the evenings. In some states contracted security guards are regulated. It is important to know the intensity of the credentialing process for contracted security as well as the reputation of the selected agency. Finally, a service to escort users from the building to their cars would convince library users that the library is serious about security.

Landscaping

While landscaping can be a beautiful addition to the appearance of any library, it must also be designed or improved with security in mind. Trees and shrubs should be placed to provide shade without offering hiding places. Access to the parking lots and external book drops should also be free and clear. Trees should not extend close to and as high as windows that open—so that people cannot exit or enter by climbing a tree. Some libraries have eliminated outdoor book drops in order to enhance security. Freestanding, drive-up book drops that allow borrowers to return books after hours without getting out of their cars are increasingly popular for users. Unfortunately, these same convenient book drops present safety risks for the library employees who have to empty them the next business day.

Windows, Doors, Keys, Locks

The legitimate possible points of entry into the building need to be the most secure. Windows and non-public doors need to be locked. Public entrances should be clearly marked. Some libraries use human monitors at the public entrances. These monitors may be contracted security officers or police. Monitors check the identification cards of registered borrowers or require registration for others. Called "access management," this system creates as much a sense of security as many other interventions. In some situations librarians believe the appearance of security is often as effective as real security. (Robison, Marshall, and Cravey, 1992: 164)

There should be no extant keys to the fire and emergency exits. Other keys should be restricted to only a few employees and accountability for those keys should be made routine.

Libraries that have converted to card access systems are finding that such systems provide less security than human monitors. Often staff (for expediency) will admit others with their card. A good human monitor will not admit anyone without proper authorization. A system must be developed with a human monitor for situations when otherwise authorized persons forget their authorization card. In a card access system, one usually just shares another cardholder's information and gains immediate access. This system may work in a small library where everyone knows what is going on. However, in a large library where many people do not know each other, people who do not belong, for one reason or another, may gain easy access to a building with an unmonitored card access system. Layne (1994b) reports that one of the first things he finds when assessing security breaches is a casual regard for the card access system. Frequently he observes people admitting others who do not have such a card. With a card access system, all persons entering the building should use their own card or the system is compromised.

Rest Room Access

While the idea of free access to rest rooms is the norm, there may be some rationale for securing rest rooms and requiring users to request a key. One library has loaded keys into their online circulation system as "items" with a standard loan period. Borrowers must "check out" keys just as they would check out books. The loan period can be reasonable enough to permit appropriate access. The advantage of this system is that the rest rooms are limited to known borrowers and access can be more easily controlled. Public libraries, in order to eliminate the threats of legal actions, might also need a system for allowing unregistered users access to the rest rooms. This system could be accomplished by requiring a sign out/in sheet for the keys or by requiring rest room users to register as library users. Certainly, this solution would work best in a small library with a limited number of rest rooms available to the public.

Building Design

Ideally the building will have been designed with security and safety in mind. For most libraries, however, such topics as capacity and service were the primary issues considered when buildings were designed. There are many ways older building can be retooled for safety, however. Police emergency phones can be placed strategically throughout the building. Intercom systems can be added. A building walk-through will reveal nooks and crannies where problems could occur. Good-faith efforts can be made to eliminate these problem areas by adding shelving or by building storage closets, for example. What is sacrificed in seating or shelving capacity is well worth the peace of mind in knowing that the building is safer. As use of the building evolves, additional problem areas will appear. These areas can be dealt with individually. Stairwells are a particular problem and would benefit from the expensive solution of a monitoring system.

Building Core

The core of the building should not be ignored for safety concerns. The larger and more complex the library building, the greater the potential for dangerous situations. One library had a building patrol. One staff member and a few temporary employees would walk through the building each week. They were looking for lights that were burned out, broken pieces of tile that might present a safety hazard, metal range finders that were askew, shelves that seemed insecure, and other safety issues. They were also able to identify areas that needed additional shelving attention or areas that were sites for problem behaviors. Once these latter sites were identified, they could be fixed by increasing security patrols, by rearranging shelving, or by other means.

Sight Lines to the Stacks

While it is not always possible to have a direct sight line to and through the stacks, that is the safest building design. It would be particularly important in a small library, or one that is staffed at night by only one person, that the sight lines to the stacks not include any invisible areas. When users know they can be watched, they are less likely to get into trouble.

Eating, Drinking, Smoking

Food and drink create safety hazards that are health related. For example, spills and food wrappers attract bugs, contribute to falls, and can damage books, media, and computer terminals. Some libraries prohibit food and drink from being brought into the library. One library located in a warm climate offers a covered vending area just outside the main entrance but does not permit food inside the library. Some libraries permit beverages inside the facility as long as they are in spill-proof containers. Other libraries provide lounges as places for food consumption and then prohibit eating throughout the rest of the building. It is very difficult to monitor food consumption within the library and doing so has the potential for creating ill will. In an interesting twist, one undergraduate library designed the stacks around a food court and noticed no increase in food-related trash in the stacks. Reading was encouraged in the food court!

For building safety, prohibiting smoking will decrease the chance of fires inside the building. Some states and jurisdictions are now prohibiting smoking in all public buildings. The best suggestion is that even if a particular state does not do this, the library should prohibit smoking. A second best alternative would be to create a smoking room. This room would need extra ventilation independent from the main ventilation system. It should have an extra sprinkler system, as well. Cleaning such a room can become a problem, as many people do not want to clean smoke-filled rooms.

PERSONAL SAFETY

Personal safety is the second element of the kind of safe library environment that users and staff expect. Once the details of building security are worked out, issues related to a variety of personal safety concerns should be analyzed. Considerations of personal safety include emergency and disaster preparedness, patron behavior, and preemployment screening.

EMERGENCY AND DISASTER PREPAREDNESS

Much is already written on emergency and disaster preparedness in terms of library buildings, archives and special collections, and general collections. (Brand, 1984; George, 1994; Kahn, 1998; O'Neill, 1998; Shuman, 1999; Alire, 2000) Little specific information seems to be written about the safety of users and employees during these situations. However, "preparedness" is the key word. The same kind of energy that went into planning to protect expensive collections needs to go into assuring the safety of users and employees. Plans must be in place for natural disasters, environmental concerns, fire preparedness, health emergencies, and bomb threats.

Natural Disasters

Many natural disasters are site-specific. For example, libraries in the tornado belt will have different plans from those in the hurricane states. The general idea for managing these problems is the same, however. Site-specific natural disaster issues to consider are tornado, hurricanes, floods, severe rain or snowstorms, earthquakes or tremors, and the like. Obviously, if the library is situated in a state where these events are common, there will likely already be a plan not to open on a day when these events are predicted. What about times when these events occur during the day or without prediction? At what point is the building evacuated? Which employees are expected to remain and how will the library assure their safety? What about disasters that occur on weekends and during evenings when staff and patrons may already be at the library?

Responsible administrators are aware not only of weekend and evening staff, but also of those few staff who must arrive 30 to 60 minutes ahead of time to prepare the building for opening and those staff who usually stay beyond closing to assure the building is properly secured. In large metropolitan areas, the responsible administrator will have a sense of how far these people live from the library and can factor that information into the decision making. In one university library, the director knew what time the earliest arriving staff member left home in the morning. The director made sure the campus administrators understood that the decision to "not open" in a potential emergency could not be left until normal office hours. This director was able to get university officials to make such decisions by 6 A.M., so that staff members, expecially those with a 45–minute commute, would not arrive on time only to be told to return home. The entire library staff benefited from this "heads up" approach to emergency planning.

Circulation departments are frequently the places where staff must remain to assist in closing the building. In one library, circulation staff took up a collection and amassed enough money to stock one roll each of nickels, dimes, and quarters. This money is stored in the departmental safe and is then moved to an accessible place during the severe weather season. Its purpose is simply to "be available" in the event of an emergency that might strand an employee in the building. The money can then be used for vending machines in case a staff member is unable to get out of the building. This creative plan emerged when a severe snowstorm forced the closing of the library and the entire metropolitan area at about noon on a weekday. One staff member, who depended on her husband for a ride home, remained in the library until well after midnight. The husband had been caught in evacuation traffic after he first picked up their children at school. He could not get to his wife and she had no money even to purchase a snack. The rule for this emergency fund is that coins must be replaced in the same form, so there are always three rolls of coins available for the next emergency.

Environmental Concerns

Environmental concerns may include hazardous chemicals in the workplace, airborne pathogens, the building's ventilation system, "funny" smells, and air pollution. A staff member should be appointed to represent the library as the environmental officer. This person should attend training classes on these topics and should be the point of contact for such emergencies. Someone also needs to represent the library when it is open in the evenings and on weekends.

Hazardous chemicals in the workplace are becoming a concern of professional safety officials. Surprisingly, such things as liquid paper, office machinery cleaning fluids, and liquids used by the custodial staff to clean the building may be dangerous in large quantities. Airborne pathogens may be closely linked to the heating and ventilation system for the library. These systems should be cleaned regularly and evaluated for proper functioning. Temperatures that fluctuate too much and air that is too hot or too dry can be detrimental to people as well as to computers and books. Thermographs and other sophisticated gear are available to evaluate air within the building. Plans should also be in place to deal with situations that result in a seriously uncomfortable building environment. When is a building so hot it must be evacuated and closed?

In some metropolitan areas, mandated air pollution abatement programs are leading to commuting plans that allow flexible work schedules, assistance in arranging carpools, telecommuting, and shifting from single-occupant vehicles to other forms of transportation. Again, a staff member might need to be appointed to coordinate the library's efforts to support such programs. Administrators should be aware that staff with severe asthma and other respiratory disorders might have special needs.

Fire Preparedness

Most institutions already have information in place about how to evacuate the building and who is responsible for what duties. In many libraries, these plans are practiced with fire drills. In some libraries the plans are tested by frequent "prank" fire alarms. It is important to remember that for fire preparedness, every alarm must be treated as the real thing. It is good to have planned, unannounced fire drills. Also, fire drills should occur in all types of typical weather—not just when the temperature is moderate. Among the issues to consider in fire drills are directing users through the building to the exits and assisting users and staff on upper floors who cannot use the stairs. Opening all exits and entrances to speed egress and keeping people far enough away from the entrances so they will not be endangered are also important elements. Finally, it is critical to coordinate the "all clear" signal.

Ideally the library will work closely and regularly with the appropriate fire marshal to assure that the building and its evacuation plans comply with local ordinances. Most likely, the library's fire alarm system will be tied directly to a local fire or police department. When this link occurs, library staff need only be concerned with what should be done in the few minutes prior to the arrival of the fire department. Quick-acting staff can turn off the electronic theft-detection system and open all doors so they become exits. Staff and users who will need assistance getting out of the building should know the evacuation plan. In one library, these people are advised to go to the stairwells and wait. Staff members who are able to use the stairs then report to a central person the location of people needing such assistance. Staff should be trained not to try to carry an occupied wheelchair or a person with a mobility challenge down the stairs.

Once the fire department arrives, however, fire officials should be told who is in charge and to whom they should report the "all clear." They should also be told of people waiting in stairwells. Library staff should not attempt to assist fire or police officials once they are on the scene. In a fire emergency, the appropriate local officials take over the management of the building until they turn it back over to the library official. Additionally, staff should not be expected to assist in any way other than for those first few minutes. It is unreasonable to expect staff to be endangered to save collections or buildings.

Health Emergencies

Staff should be trained in the most modern techniques for dealing with a variety of health emergencies. This does not mean that staff should treat these situations. Bleeding injuries, seizures, heart attacks, and other medical emergencies should result in a direct call to the local emergency number. Staff should be willing to call for emergency assistance and should know how to describe the situation. A cup of water or a seat in an office can be offered. A folding screen or a human shield can be used for privacy for seriously ill persons. Again, the response time from the local emergency crew should be fast. Staff intervention will only be required for a short time.

After the response team has arrived, staff may be required to deal with curious bystanders. Out of respect for the person having the emergency, very little should be said. "The paramedics have taken him to the hospital," should be sufficient. Information beyond that violates the person's right to privacy.

While it is tempting to offer a colleague an over-the-counter pain reliever, this should not be done—for colleagues or for users. The risk of personal liability or liability for the library is great. Bandages can be offered for a small cut, but it is best for the person to seek medical attention. In one college, a library that once had a fully stocked first-aid kit now directs students and employees to the campus health center. At least one public services staff member should be appointed as a source of health information. The selected staff member should attend such classes as a current-awareness course on body fluid–borne pathogens. Attendance is not to train the library staff member as a paramedic, but to convey the risks involved in treating medical situations.

Library books found with vomit, ejaculate, excrement, or other body fluids should be withdrawn immediately from the collection. If staff must handle these books they should do so with protective gloves. Procedures should be developed to streamline the withdrawal process so as few people as possible actually touch these damaged books.

It is helpful to have protective gloves, a wheelchair, an extra chair, a folding cot, a privacy screen, and antibacterial soap available in a public service location.

Bomb Threats

Bomb threats seem to be on the increase. Staff should be trained how to respond to bomb threats that come to a departmental telephone. Staff should be aware that, in some cases, a telephone call or an evacuation alarm or announcement could trigger an explosion. The police will give directions for notifying departments and clearing the building. In addition, there should be an evacuation plan for the building.

Bomb threats always should be taken seriously! After evacuation for a bomb threat, it can take an hour or more to evaluate a building for a bomb. Staff should quickly grab personal belongings—such as keys, briefcases, lunches, purses—in case the evacuation is an extended one. However, the retrieval of these items should in no way delay the evacuation. Staff should have a meeting place in a building a safe distance from the library which will serve as the central place for information. Just as for fire emergencies, a plan should be in place to disengage an electronic book-theft-detection system and open all entrances and exits to speed up egress. One library person should be known as the central source of all information for staff and users, and no one should be permitted to return to a building without approval from that official. A backup should be appointed and be well known to staff for night and weekend emergencies.

PATRON BEHAVIOR

Much has been written about the "difficult" patron. (Shuman, 1984; Salter and Salter, 1988; Smith, 1994; McNeil and Johnson, 1996; Shuman, 1999; Rubin, 2000) Like beauty, "degree of difficulty" of a patron is often in the eyes of the beholder. However, examples of problem patron behavior include:

- Emotionally disturbed people
- Verbally aggressive patrons
- Panhandlers
- Sexual deviants
- Exhibitionists
- Proselytizers
- People whose behavior is altered by the use of addictive substances
- Loiterers
- Library users who are angry, irate, physically threatening or verbally assaulting

Employees who have received training in how to defuse a difficult situation verbally can defuse many "problem behaviors." Sometimes just conferring with a colleague (as opposed to referring the patron to someone else) is enough to convince the patron that he or she is being heard. Such attention frequently has a calming effect. However, staff should be trained to call the local authorities quickly if they feel endangered. Library administrators need to understand that feeling endangered is a personal response that they can neither mandate nor change simply by becoming angry at the staff member. Rubin (2000: 23–50) offers 20 basic strategies for defusing the angry patron. These strategies, including listening, validating, breathing, and treating the user with respect, are critical for any potentially difficult public service exchange. In addition, specialized training and experience may extend a specific staff member's willingness or ability to deal with problem behaviors.

Local law enforcement agencies, however, have employees who are specifically trained for behavioral emergencies. These agencies should be called quickly to intervene. In addition, library users cannot be expected to handle such threatening situations. Users expect library staff to keep them safe. Frequently, frightened or endangered users will report a problem to staff at a public service desk. These staff should accept the users' word for the difficulty of a situation and proceed with caution. Written library policies should address in detail what kinds of library staff responses are appropriate and what situations require law enforcement agency intervention. The best plan is to err on the side of calling law enforcement, rather than risking injury to a user or to a staff member.

Occasionally staff members have personal problems that follow them to work. Credit companies frequently track people to their workplaces, and they make many telephone calls to them. Even if the staff members have done an otherwise excellent job of keeping their private lives away from the workplace, these callers create anger among supervisors, fear for the employees, and frustration for the telephone receptionists. Sometimes a manager can talk to these people and tell them that their repeated phone calls must stop. Generally, this tactic is effective. Staff members may be stalked. Patrons, former sweethearts, or angry spouses are often the stalkers. These people also frequently call the workplace and want to talk to the person. If the person is not there, the caller typically becomes angry or abusive with the person answering the telephone. The caller may ask for the person's work schedule. Staff members who work alone at night may really be in danger and the library should do whatever is possible to protect these people. One library department refuses to give out work schedules for any staff member. If the patron is insistent, the supervisor's schedule may be given. An attempt can be made to divert the call to someone on duty rather than giving out the schedule. Departmental supervisors, however, are told in the job interview that their work schedules will be given out upon patron request.

PREEMPLOYMENT SCREENING

The latest hot button in library safety is preemployment screening. (Campus Crime Prevention Programs, 1992: 1–10; Layne, 1994a) Administrators will ask, "If you can't trust your own employees, who can you trust?"; thus a mechanism is needed to assure that new employees are trustworthy. Traditionally, businesses have long used all sorts of preemployment screening. Such screening includes ability testing (typing tests, for example), intelligence tests, personality tests, scenario questionnaires (what would you do if . . . ?), drug tests, credit checks, criminal background checks, daily performance tests (video simulators for bus drivers, for example), and handwriting analysis. Lie detector tests are no longer legal as a preemployment screening device. One reason businesses use such a wide variety of tests is that they lose upwards of $40 billion annually to employee theft, vandalism, and bribery. (Bassman, 1992: 114) Another reason for preemployment testing is the increase in negligent hiring actions. Bassman defines negligent hiring actions as those where the company or organization is "liable for an employee's harmful behavior toward a customer or fellow employee on the grounds that the company could have taken steps to avoid hiring a person who would be likely to do such harm." (Bassman, 1992: 107) Before an intensive or invasive system of preemployment screening is implemented, legal advice and administrative buy-in should be obtained. Tests should be relevant to specific job duties. For example, credit checks and criminal background investigations might be appropriate for staff members who handle money. Criminal background checks would be important for children's department workers. Daily video-performance tests could be important for shuttle drivers or operators of vans that travel from library to library delivering requested items in a public library system or consortium. Circular reasoning is to blame when hiring officials decide that because they selected the candidate, there is nothing "wrong" with that person. If the new employee is a stranger with whom the hiring official "clicked" in the interview, there is still nothing to suggest that applicant is any more trustworthy than any other stranger. Also, it is important to remember that events in the library or personal events can impact an employee's behavior. For example, in one library the stress of completing a project by a deadline led one staff member to threaten to hit another on the head with a computer keyboard. Both staff members were well behaved, quality employees who got caught up in a difficult situation. Since the keyboard was attached to the terminal, the incident was over before anything other than threats ensued. In another library, a temporary employee distraught over not being selected to fill a full-time vacancy, returned to the library, scratched abusive remarks into the paint of the metal shelving, and then threatened to kill himself. Would preemployment screening have uncovered the potential for this behavior? If personality testing had uncovered this bent, would it have been legal to refuse to hire based on personality testing? Again, strong legal advice on the use of and interpretation of these tests is required. Legal issues related to hiring are covered in more depth in Chapter 7.

The scope of building security and personal safety is enormous. Sometimes it seems that as soon as one problem is resolved, another appears. Library staff in the forefront of security monitoring activities can feel like the "little Dutch boy" with his finger in the dike. Sometimes they feel that they are running out of fingers! However, an initial expenditure of time and talent can produce a security foundation that is prepared internally and is relevant to each library. An added advantage is that the internal creation of meaningful policy statements is not too expensive. Also, as the need arises and the times change, components can be added or deleted easily.

TYPES OF SOLUTIONS

Numerous solutions exist for personal security concerns in libraries. These solutions can be categorized as low-, medium-, and high-intensity solutions. Solutions can also be low-cost, medium-cost, or high-cost. Solutions can range from policy statements to video surveillance; from performance tests to drug testing. It is important to remain flexible and to design a variety of security solutions that can be adapted over time. Within the context of each library's unique locale and needs, budget will probably be the deciding factor in selecting appropriate options. Undergirding any security solution, however, must be a series of policy statements. Such statements anchor the low-intensity, as well as the low-cost, solution possibilities.

LOW-INTENSITY SOLUTIONS: POLICY STATEMENTS

When looking for low-intensity solutions, policy statements are the obvious first choice. A variety of statements can be devised. They can be posted, placed as bookmarks in books that are charged, included in handbooks, or any combination of these and other options. Whatever way is chosen to present these policy statements to the users, the policies need also to be readily available in an administrative manual. Policy statements should have the approval of the legal arm that represents the library and the buy-in of the local enforcement unit. Staff may be uncomfortable enforcing some types of security solutions. In these cases, the library should decide what is tolerable and what will be tolerated. There is a cause-and-effect relationship between behaviors and outcomes. For example, while having staff admonish individuals who are eating in the library is an effective way to stop such eating, it creates situations that are uncomfortable for most staff members. The library might be willing to tolerate some food eating within the library in order to keep staff from having to do "food patrols."

> ### Figure 3.1: Inclusive Policy Statement
>
> It is the policy of [Library] to maintain an atmosphere conducive to reading, study, and research. Library . . . users must refrain from exceeding acceptable noise levels, eating, drinking, and use of tobacco except in officially designated locations, and/or from any other disruptive behavior which impinges on the rights and needs of others.

Examples of policy statements that are used to undergird security of staff and users are those that address patron behavior, the library environment, hostility and aggression, threatening behavior, harassment, voyeurism, and theft of personal property. A different approach to policy statements is to have an inclusive policy statement for all library users.

Patron Behavior

A policy statement on patron behavior is important for successful library operations for two reasons. First, it protects users and staff from inappropriate or abusive actions of others. Second, it prescribes an action plan for dealing with each situation. Because the plan is in writing it assures all users are treated equitably. For example, with such a plan in place, compliant patrons' rights are protected. As well, the rights of difficult patrons are clear. (Morrissett, 1996) Rubin (2000: 84) suggests policy statements for user behavior should:

- Focus on behavior, not on people
- Be specific
- Apply to all users rather than specific groups
- Apply to behavior only on library property
- Mirror the library's mission, values, philosophy, and purpose
- Provide an avenue for appeal

Inclusive policy statements can be very succinct and specific; they need not be long. For example, consider the excerpt in Figure 3.1 from a comprehensive and brief policy statement from Western Kentucky University. (Morrissett, 1996: 146–148) This policy statement continues with a list of steps that will be taken if such behavior occurs and a list of examples of unacceptable behavior.

The Library Environment

The Detroit Public Library has a policy statement that is both more "user-friendly" and more comprehensive to the entire library environment than the Western Kentucky University policy. It begins "Your cooperation is requested in refraining from" and then lists numerous behaviors that are to be avoided. (Shuman, 1999: 76–77) The prohibited behaviors include:

- Smoking
- Drinking all types of beverages
- Leaving children unattended
- Playing loud music
- Using typewriters
- Loitering
- Sleeping
- Gambling
- Soliciting
- Campaigning
- Playing electronic devices of all types without headphones
- Fighting
- Running
- Eating
- Using obscene language
- Using abusive language
- Bringing in all but service animals
- Dressing inappropriately
- Carrying weapons or dangerous items
- Engaging in sexual acts or deviant behavior
- Mutilating library property or collections
- Using chemical substances

While the above information is clear, this statement and others like it could be improved by spelling out some of the consequences of violating the code. Even a blanket statement ("Offenses may be treated according to the most stringent local ordinance.") would improve the library's ability to enforce the document.

There are two main problems with lists of prohibited behaviors, however. The first is that the list may become quickly outdated by changes in technology, fashion, and culture. The Detroit Public Library list, however, is an excellent example of language not likely to become outdated too quickly. As a matter of policy, lists like these should be reviewed annually to assure they are still relevant and inclusive. The second problem with such lists of unacceptable behaviors is that people may be challenged to misbehave in ways not included on the list. These people then challenge the authority of the librarian on grounds that they were not breaking any of the named infractions. The regulating agency for the library may wish also to add a disclaimer to the list of acceptable or unacceptable behaviors. For example, Crimmin (1984: 27) makes the suggestion shown in Figure 3.2.

Figure 3.2: Disclaimer Statement

The posting of these specific rules "does not permit, license, or condone any act forbidden under federal law, the statutes of the state, or the ordinances of the city."

Hostility and Aggression

Hostility is "an attitude rather than a feeling." (Smith, 1994: 50) Library users who are hostile may not be angry. They may not act out their hostility. They may just use the library, not have a pleasant attitude, but never really be problem patrons. Consistent pleasant exchanges at the public service points of the library may go a long way toward calming the hostile patron. While hostile patrons are not always pleasant to deal with, there really is neither a need nor a way to provide policy statements regulating these users' attitudes. Employees' manuals may legitimately make reference to staff attitudes, however. Expectations for staff should be to serve external and internal customers with a pleasant attitude.

Aggression, on the other hand, is a behavioral problem. By nature, aggression is "an action or behavior against another, performed with the intention of doing harm." (Smith, 1994: 50) Library policy statements should include mention of persons exhibiting aggressive behavior. Staff should know acceptable strategies for dealing with these people.

Threatening Behavior

It is also important to recognize the difference between aggressive verbal behavior and aggressive behavior involving a weapon or threat of physical violence. (Smith, 1994: 67) These latter cases should be treated in a policy statement dealing with other types of unacceptable behavior. For example, if a user or a colleague is armed (even with a keyboard) and threatening, there is neither need nor time to decide if that person is angry or hostile, serious or "just kidding." For this reason, all policy statements should be backed up by references to the statute or law that the offensive behavior violates. In many jurisdictions, even the use of "fighting words" may be a violation of an ordinance or law.

Harassment

Several types of harassment occur in libraries. Categories include harassment related to gender, age, sexual orientation, ethnicity, dress, and other human differences. Harassment may take several forms including words, gestures, letters or notes, drawings, photographs, Internet screens, telephone calls, and others. A policy statement should outline the consequences of harassing behavior, such as removal from the site for users or suspension or termination for staff. Many locales require that separate harassment policies and procedures be posted in prominent locations. These statements may be required to contain the following elements:

- Definitions of harassment
- Statements of the library's philosophy of harassment
- Steps for filing a complaint
- Information on how a complaint will be handled
- Examples of prohibited conduct
- A summary statement about possible outcomes
- Information about staff training
- An explanation of how information regarding harassment will be disseminated (Johnson, 1996: 107)

Harassment policies and procedures may have to be posted. If that is the case, posters for staff and posters for users may need to be of different designs. Each poster should include the above elements that are specific only to the target group. For example, prohibited conduct for office space and public areas will probably have some differences. As well, posters should reflect the specific steps individuals from each group should follow in filing a complaint.

Voyeurism

Voyeurism is more difficult to deal with than harassment because the perpetrator can easily say that the victim's perception is incorrect. There is usually no evidence of such acts and frequently the victim is embarrassed to report the incident. Policy statements should include mention of the penalties for such activities. In some libraries, it is appropriate to have the victim report suspected actions to the circulation or reference desks. Frequently then a staff member can go to the site and inspect. A call to the police to have an identification check of the subject may yield information about the suspect's motive for being in the library. If the person is not an authorized user, the police can issue a criminal trespass warning. That means the next time the person is spotted in the library, an arrest can be made for trespassing. It is important to be careful to believe the victim as well as to afford the suspect respect. For example, it is easier to have a person removed from the premises as an unauthorized user than as a voyeur. It is also critical to recognize that same-gender voyeurism is very real and persons reporting that type of behavior must be treated with respect.

Figure 3.3: Draft Workplace Violence Policy

It is the policy of this library to maintain a safe workplace, free from any threat of physical violence, emotional abuse, or any form of intimidation. Employees, patrons, vendors, or any visitors to the facility are prohibited from bringing any type of weapon, explosive, or destructive material onto library property. Employees will not possess any of the above while engaged in library business. Any acts of vandalism, sabotage, or the threat of such acts will not be tolerated. Employees are advised to report any acts or threats of acts which are described by this policy to their immediate supervisor. Employees may report such acts by calling _____ . All complaints, reports, or advisements will be thoroughly investigated. Failure to comply with this policy is a direct violation of library rules and may result in activation of disciplinary procedures up to and including termination of employment. Where criminal violations have occurred, the library will file criminal charges and follow through with prosecution of those involved. This policy is adopted for the mutual protection of all employees and visitors. (Layne, 1994b, [12])

Theft of Personal Property

Libraries are terrific places from which to make quite a haul in personal belongings. In university libraries there is a market in textbooks. Textbooks are stolen and quickly returned to the campus bookstore for a "refund." In all libraries there is ample opportunity to steal a wide variety of items. Library users seem to be oblivious to the reality that unattended personal belongings are very likely to be stolen from any public place. While policy statements are appropriate for would-be thieves, there is also room for intensive educational programs alerting users to lurking dangers. Would a customer leave a laptop computer on a chair in a bus station for "just a minute while I go to the rest room"? Absolutely not! Why are libraries different? Signs and posters can be useful to alert users to the possibility of theft of their personal property. Such signs can also alert thieves to the library's aggressive approach to apprehending them.

Inclusive Policy Statement

Inclusive statements, long or short, are probably the most appropriate for posting. They can be backed up in an administrative manual with definitions, outcomes, and statements of legality. Layne Consultants International has developed a sample of such an inclusive statement (see Figure 3.3). The intent is that the statement for the public will be posted and that staff members sign individual copies. The signed staff copy then becomes a part of the employee's permanent personnel file. Vendors are also bound by this policy.

No matter what types of policy statements are selected, or how they are displayed, there is no point in a policy statement that is "on paper only." If the administration or the local enforcement units are unwilling or unable to enforce the policy statement, it is worthless. If staff members are unwilling or unable to follow through on the written procedures, the documents will be ignored.

MEDIUM-INTENSITY SOLUTIONS: TRAINING

Training is a solution of medium intensity. It also has medium-sized costs associated with it. There are many types of training programs, including those for employees, patrons, and security personnel.

Employee Awareness Training

Training staff to deal with problems or to implement the security plan is critical to the success of the plan. During an incident, it is important to act quickly and from a position of intellectual and emotional strength. Library employees should be able to "analyze the situation, respond quickly, choose a proper site for the confrontation, bring a back-up, think of safety, and be non-threatening." (Salter and Salter, 1988: 131) Proper training leads to the ability to analyze the situation quickly and to determine the best response. Although role-playing is not the most popular training tool from the trainee's perspective, it is an excellent way to demonstrate appropriate behavior. Role-playing is especially useful for reviewing difficult situations, because in such situations the human stress response may kick in, causing the employee either to fail to react or to react inappropriately. Lots of training can mask the fear response and propel the employee into appropriate action. Of course, time must be provided for the employee to talk about the "success" of the experience after it is over.

As important as a nonthreatening encounter is the need for backup. Encounters that could become disagreeable require a backup. No difficult situation should be undertaken alone. There should also be a backup plan in place for obtaining help. For example, in the previous case of the terminated employee, he returned the next day to demand his job back. The department head and the employee's supervisor agreed to meet with him the following morning. Once the three were settled in a glass-walled conference room, the employee pulled out a knife, held it to his throat, and threatened to kill himself unless he was rehired. The department head had sensed something could go very wrong in the meeting and had a third staff member strategically placed outside the office. When the knife came out, the department head stood up and knocked on the glass wall. The hidden staff member called the police who arrived quickly to settle the situation and obtain counseling for the troubled ex-employee. This confrontation was successful because all participants were very experienced in dealing with problem behaviors and worked comfortably together—even in the absence of details of the problem. Also, the local police were familiar with the staff and knew that the call, even without the customary details, was critical.

The benefits of a well-trained staff are many. They include benefits to the users, staff, and governing agencies. (Salter and Salter, 1988: 129–141) Users benefit from excellent staff training because they are safer when the staff know what they are doing. Users feel safer when rules are enforced and when staff handle themselves competently. Users with mental health problems also get the help they need if the behavior plan is well conceived and well implemented. Staff benefit from excellent training because they feel more confident, are more competent, can implement the plan without fear of costly errors (such as law suits), and can apply the lessons learned to their daily lives. Library governance benefits from employees who are well trained to defuse difficult situations; training is expensive, but there is less staff turnover when staff are empowered to respond to difficult situations. Training for difficult situations should include procedures for such people as a troubled coworker or user, a person with abusive language or threats, and workplace violence.

Paris (1984: 80–82) provides an outline of topics to consider in developing an extensive in-service training program. Topics include written policies, tours of the facilities, demonstrations of the operation of protection equipment, and presentations on the major security problems of that library and how to resolve them. Training should include on-the-job training as well as specific and tailored off-site training. Seminars, workshops, and simulations are useful training tools. Training for security should be viewed as a long-term investment in an ongoing project. Circumstances change, the environment may change, and the problems will differ. Consequently, training must stay relevant to each library. The Public Library Association developed a formalized checklist for analyzing training needs. Training needs of all types, including safety and security, can be identified with this form. (Nelson, Altman, and Mayo, 2000: 68–69)

User Training

User training for security purposes is an interesting concept—the user must want to be trained. Frequently users do not have time for this sort of training. They depend on the library staff to keep them safe, and they do not perceive the dangers in the library. Somehow users must be informed of what can happen in the library, and what they can do about it, without unnecessarily alarming them. Users can be instructed about what is and is not appropriate behavior. They can learn how and where to report problems. If such training can take place with a library staff member in the training role, safety can be enhanced. As the users learn to recognize more staff faces, they will feel freer to seek assistance from library staff. At least, signs should be posted alerting users to keep track of their personal property and to report problems to library staff or at public service desks.

Training of Institutional Security Personnel

It may seem odd that the library could or should train security personnel, but such training is necessary. Security personnel should know the mission of the library and the library's positions on issues related to its security. The same sort of training plan suggested by Paris for library employees is also appropriate for training institutional security personnel. Some libraries use temporary employees for security, some use contracted security firms, and others use police. Each of these security options has a specific role, clear-cut rights and responsibilities, and a set of legal duties. Regardless of the option chosen, the security personnel should get to know the building and the clientele of the library they serve. Usually they are pleased to receive such site-specific training. If security personnel balk at such specific training, they are probably the wrong choice for the library. State credentialing requirements for contracted security vary substantially. It is a good idea to understand the regulations for credentialing security guards in the library's home state prior to selecting that option.

HIGH-INTENSITY SOLUTIONS: PEOPLE AND ELECTRONICS

In order for a high-intensity (high-cost) solution to be effective, it must be both meaningful and visible. People, electronics, and creative ideas form the basis of these solutions.

Increased Security Presence

The addition of security guards, patrols, or police may enhance security of an institution. The cost is high and is continuous. When this type of security is considered, the enormous ramifications on the library's overall budget should always be reviewed. There are a variety of ways and combinations of choices available in order to increase the security presence in a library. Depending on the type of library, contract security, staff patrols, temporary employees, and local police in an overtime mode are all obvious choices. Having additional staff work late hours and weekends would also contribute to a more visible staff security presence. Additional staff would certainly make the library "feel" safer for both staff and users. Finally, making the commitment never to have one sole staff member on duty would go a long way toward enhancing staff security as well as that of the users. The latter two suggestions also involve long-term funding commitments.

Electronic Surveillance Systems

Electronic surveillance systems meet both the meaningful and visible criteria. These systems can include closed-circuit television and some of the other building solutions mentioned in the previous chapter. Not only does this solution require the high-cost installation of an electronic system; the maintenance and the monitoring of the system will be a continuing expense. Since it does little good to invest in a complex and expensive surveillance system if it will not be monitored closely, additional uses for the system might justify its purchase despite the high cost. For example, an access management/visitor control point has several advantages. The most obvious advantage is that this arrangement quickly conveys to the visitor that the library is serious about security.

Increased Office Control

Along with electronic security devices to control the doors and the stacks, offices, staff lounges, and public service desks should be monitored. Staff in the traditional technical services offices should receive ample protection from intruders. The use of swipe cards, proximity cards, and fingerprint technology is increasing in popularity for protecting office areas. Videotaping transactions at the service desks is another popular way to keep problem patrons from taking charge and intimidating staff. In addition, videotapes are a good training tool for individual staff to see their own successes and mistakes. To protect the library from lawsuits and to respect individuals' privacy, videotapes should be shown to others only with written permission of those videotaped. Caller ID on the telephone may discourage harassing telephone calls; announced monitoring of telephone calls creates even greater security.

Creative Problem Solving

"There are many ways to skin a cat," so the saying goes. The same is true about security. Staff and patron brainstorming yield terrific ideas. Security teams empowered to investigate pricing issues yield good solutions couched in a fiscally responsible frame. Security teams also net a comprehensive understanding of "why" certain solutions are uncomfortable or impractical. Creative problem solving that involves the library's patron audience also allows members of the served community to think of fund-raising opportunities for Friends groups, grants to be written, or capital campaigns.

SUMMARY

It is important to think of personal and human security as separate from security of the collections and building. Among the things libraries need to look at for assuring user and staff safety is the compatibility between library policies and those of the local legal system. Libraries cannot develop policies and procedures in a vacuum. Governing documents must be developed with governing bodies in mind. In many cases, such as in school or academic libraries, appropriate behavior throughout the parent system is detailed in a handbook. Behavior in the library should conform to the same handbook guidelines. Posting the guidelines presents a difficult conundrum. In some legal jurisdictions, in order to enforce them, guidelines must be posted. In other jurisdictions, this is not the case. Some librarians and users balk at the idea of posting guidelines, fearing that doing so casts the library in a negative way. Legal counsel should approve any newly developed guidelines. (Salter and Salter, 1988: 124)

It is important to think, too, in terms of individual rights and responsibilities when designing security configurations and training programs. As a base from which to expand planning for behavioral security programs, Caputo's (1984: 25) five rights and responsibilities of all people are classic. She asserts that all people have the right to be respected, to "feel," to make mistakes, to say "no," and to ask questions. Conversely, all people have the responsibility to respect others, to accept their feelings, to accept their mistakes, to accept "no" as an appropriate answer, and to accept questions from others. Specifically, Caputo (1984: 26–28) continues with librarians and users' library rights and their implicit responsibilities. Librarians have the right, among other rights, to dislike a patron, the right to expect respect of library property, and the right to understand what is expected of them in different work situations. This latter right is especially important in implementing a user and staff security program. Policies governing such a program need to include clearly defined expectations for staff behavior. Training must be continuous. In addition, a method is needed to inform users of the program and what they should do to keep themselves and their property safe.

Under Caputo's model (1984: 29–30), users have the additional right to expect equal treatment, not to be disturbed by others, and to dislike libraries and their processes. Also, librarians observe from monitoring behavior that users expect a safe environment. How to meet that expectation presents a challenge.

This chapter has enumerated many issues and possible solutions surrounding the topic of security to the library user and staff. This chapter has also enumerated suggestions of varying intensity and cost for meeting the security needs of users and staff. Whatever solutions are chosen should conform to local legal practices and a variety of American Library Association statements, codes, bills, and guidelines. (Larson and Totten, 1998: 149–199) The following factors are critical in designing a global system for protecting all users and staff in a library:

- Location
- Budget
- Governance
- Size and type of the library

REFERENCES

Alire, Camila, ed. 2000. *Library Disaster Planning and Recovery Handbook*. New York: Neal-Schuman.

American Library Association, Library Administration and Management Section, BES Safety and Security of Library Buildings Committee, Security Guidelines Subcommittee. 1999. "Library Security Guidelines, Draft Document, April 12, 1999." *www.ala.org/lama/ committees/bes/sslbguidelines.html*

Bassman, Emily S. 1992. *Abuse in the Workplace: Management Remedies and Bottom Line Impact*. Westport, Conn.: Quorum Books.

Brand, Marvine, ed. 1984. *Security for Libraries: People, Buildings, Collections*. Chicago: American Library Association.

Campus Crime Prevention Programs. 1992. *Library Safety and Security: A Comprehensive Manual for Library Administrators and Police and Security Officers*. Goshen, Ky.: Campus Crime Prevention Programs.

Caputo, Janette S. 1984. *The Assertive Librarian*. Phoenix: Oryx.

Crimmin, Wilbur B. 1984. "Institutional, Personal, Collection, and Building Security Concerns." In *Security for Libraries: People, Buildings, Collections*, edited by Marvine Brand. Chicago: American Library Association.

Fennelly, Lawrence J. 1989. "Designing Security with the Architects." In *Handbook of Loss Prevention and Crime Prevention*, 2d ed., edited by Lawrence J. Fennelly. Boston: Butterworths.

George, Susan C., ed. 1994. *Emergency Planning and Management in College Libraries*. Chicago: American Library Association.

Johnson, Denise J. 1996. "Sexual Harassment in the Library." In *Patron Behavior in Libraries: A Handbook of Positive Approaches to Negative Situations*, edited by Beth McNeil and Denise J. Johnson. Chicago: American Library Association.

Kahn, Miriam B. 1998. *Disaster Response and Planning for Libraries*. Chicago: American Library Association.

Larson, Jeanette, and Herman L. Totten. 1998. *Model Policies for Small and Medium Public Libraries*. New York: Neal-Schuman.

Layne, Stevan P. 1994a. *The Official Library Security Manual*. Dillon, Co.: Layne Consultants International.

———. 1994b. "Violence in the Library: Prevention, Preparedness and Response." Dillon, Co.: Layne Consultants International.

McNeil, Beth, and Denise J. Johnson, eds. 1996. *Patron Behavior in Libraries: A Handbook of Positive Approaches to Negative Situations*. Chicago: American Library Association.

Morrissett, Linda A. 1996. "Developing and Implementing a Patron Behavior Policy." In *Patron Behavior in Libraries: A Handbook of Positive Approaches to Negative Situations*, edited by Beth McNeil and Denise J. Johnson. Chicago: American Library Association.

Nelson, Sandra, Ellen Altman, and Diane Mayo for the Public Library Association. 2000. *Managing for Results: Effective Resource Allocation for Public Libraries*. Chicago: American Library Association.

O'Block, Robert L. 1989. "Environmental Design." In *Handbook of Loss Prevention and Crime Prevention*, 2d ed., edited by Lawrence J. Fennelly. Boston: Butterworths. (21–36)

O'Neill, Robert K., ed. 1998. *Management of Library and Archival Security: From the Outside Looking In*. New York: Haworth.

Paris, Janelle A. 1984. "Internal and External Responsibilities and Practices for Library Security." In *Security for Libraries: People, Buildings, Collections*, edited by Marvine Brand. Chicago: American Library Association.

Robison, Carolyn L., John D. Marshall, Jr., and Pamela J. Cravey. 1992. "Legal and Practical Aspects of Securing the General Collection in Academic Libraries." In *Academic Libraries in Urban and Metropolitan Areas: A Management Handbook*, edited by Gerard B. McCabe. New York: Greenwood Press.

Rubin, Rhea Joyce. 2000. *Defusing the Angry Patron: A How-To-Do-It Manual for Librarians and Paraprofessionals*. New York: Neal-Schuman.

Salter, Charles A., and Jeffrey L. Salter. 1988. *On the Frontlines: Coping with the Library's Problem Patrons*. Englewood, Co.: Libraries Unlimited.

Shuman, Bruce A. 1984. *River Bend Revisited: The Problem Patron in the Library*. Phoenix: Oryx.

———. 1999. *Library Security and Safety Handbook: Prevention, Policies, and Procedures*. Chicago: American Library Association.

Smith, Kitty. 1994. *Serving the Difficult Customer: A How-To-Do-It Manual for Library Staff*. New York: Neal-Schuman.

4 SECURITY OF ELECTRONIC FILES AND SYSTEMS

FUNDAMENTALS OF ELECTRONIC SECURITY

Computer security has the triple goal of physical protection of the equipment, protection against unauthorized access to the available data, and protection against unauthorized access to the programs. (Buck, 1991: 157) To achieve these goals, the basic framework for discussing computer security includes the concepts of "objectives," "vulnerabilities," and "safeguards." Literature specific to the protection of computer systems, despite location, generally begins with a discussion of these ideas. Therefore, objectives, vulnerabilities, and safeguards will be mentioned before any library-specific concerns are enumerated.

OBJECTIVES

The three fundamental objectives, or goals, of electronic security are "confidentiality," "integrity," and "availability to legitimate users." These three goals may be correctly understood both as mutually exclusive qualities and as interrelated ideas.

Confidentiality

"Confidentiality," "secrecy," and "privacy" are terms used synonymously to describe one fundamental goal of electronic security. "Confidentiality means that the assets of a computing system are accessible only by authorized parties; . . . only authorized people can see protected data." (Pfleeger, 1997: 5) Included under the confidentiality umbrella are all types of reading, viewing, printing, and storage devices. Traditional trash cans and recycling bins may also allow for breaches of confidentiality in the strictest sense.

Threats to confidentiality "attempt to disclose a user's secret or private information to an unauthorized party." (Rubin, Geer, and Ranum, 1997: 15) Successful attacks against confidentiality may result in a lack or loss of privacy. In addition, attacks may include the theft or loss of information from and about the server or the client. Also, financial information may be stolen and used to create false information about a situation. Billing for commercial services may be altered. Services may be stolen and modified for another person's commercial gain. Personal information and identities may also be stolen. Thus, another way of stating the objective of confidentiality is that "information is disclosed only according to policy." (Summers, 1997: 3)

At a more detailed level of exploration, confidentiality is further divided into "content confidentiality" and "message flow confidentiality." Both use encryption techniques to ensure confidentiality, and together they ensure that unauthorized disclosure of data does not occur. In addition, "enveloping techniques" can be used to conceal, from sophisticated traffic analysis protocols, the fact that there actually is a flow of data. (Kou, 1997:5) While interesting, these ideas and many others are outside the scope of this chapter.

Integrity

Integrity is another of the three fundamental objectives of computing security. Integrity means freedom from introduced errors. That is, the user or server data, the programs, the messages, or the memory can be modified only by authorized people in authorized ways. Also, included in this objective are the notions of "consistency," "internal consistency," "precision," "accuracy," and "appropriate results." (Pfleeger, 1997: 5–7) For example, when data, such as the annual budget, are stored, users assume the data stored are accurate. Users should rightfully be able to assume that no incorrect data have been inserted through intentional and malicious means. It is interesting that unintentional error is not usually included in this security goal.

Attacks against integrity are termed "enabling" attacks. Such attacks enable other attacks because they permit the intruder to take full or partial control of a computer. Once such control is assumed, the intruder may be able to read, modify, edit, delete, mail, and do anything else on the computer that the authorized user could do. (Rubin, Geer, and Ranum, 1997: 12–13) Another way to look at the goal of integrity is to ensure that "information is not destroyed or corrupted and that the system performs correctly." (Summers, 1997: 3)

Availability to Legitimate Users

Availability to legitimate users is the final fundamental objective of security of electronic information and equipment. Availability includes the idea of access to data, to computing resources, and to services. This goal frequently mentions "capacity," "sufficiency," and "timeliness." "Authentication" is the applications term given to the need for systems to be available to legitimate and authorized users. "Denial of service" is the phrase used to mean the opposite of availability. Systems may become unavailable due to power outages, bogus requests, viruses, full memory, full disks, and impersonation of authorized users. Another way to state the goal of availability to legitimate users is that "services are available when they are needed." (Summers, 1997: 4)

VULNERABILITIES

"Vulnerability" and "exposure" are terms used synonymously to mean a "weakness of a system that could allow security to be violated." (Summers, 1997: 5) Generally, software, hardware, and data are considered as the three main areas of computing vulnerability. Some writers may include "users" as a fourth area of vulnerability. Still others include the "portable-computing environment" as a new area of vulnerability. These areas of exposure and the places where they overlap create security risks.

Software

Software is the essence of computing. Without software, hardware and data are worthless. Traditionally, software includes operating systems, utility programs, and application programs. Provided one has the necessary keys, software can be deleted, modified, interrupted, intercepted, misplaced, copied, and sold without compensation to the owner. These events can be malicious or accidental. Software can also insert programs that cause other things to happen to existing programs.

Hardware

Hardware and its components can be stolen or destroyed. Hardware is the physical computer and its peripherals, including media storage facilities. Theft of computing time and services, disgruntled staff, and increased vulnerabilities caused by shared facilities and networks may also be included in the hardware security category. In today's offices where usually every employee has a personal computer, such machine vulnerability is great.

Data

Data are what make computer applications unique. Therefore, data may be both harder to protect and more important to safeguard. Data are often available in electronic format as well as in print, which increases data vulnerability. Data can be intercepted, interrupted, modified, created, and fabricated. These events can be purposeful, malicious, or accidental. Data can be obtained from the trash, by bribing staff, or through serendipity. Or, programs, system errors, and flawed communications protocol can compromise data. Security of data includes preventing unauthorized disclosure and modification, and preventing denial of authorized access. (Pfleeger, 1997: 9)

SAFEGUARDS

Safeguards are measures that reduce system vulnerability and risks in all types of computing environments. They are also known as "countermeasures" or "controls." The most commonly known safeguards are for software. These measures include virus protection packages, the testing of new software on stand-alone machines, encryption, and prohibiting the use of shareware in a networked environment. Safeguards for hardware may include cable locks and encasement. Encasing the hardware makes it more difficult to steal. Such protection can also help control the removal of internal components, such as network cards.

In the contemporary portable-computing environment, the vulnerabilities have expanded due to remote connectivity methods. Potential exposures in this environment still include loss, theft, and data destruction. However, the size of the problem is just being recognized. Dial-up access and the expansion of wireless networks permit still-unknown security risks. Among the safeguards currently available for off-site protection are single-use passwords and user education. (Maier, 1999)

The interactions between the threats, the vulnerabilities, and the safeguards create the framework for understanding the need for computer security, despite the applications environment. How, then, can this information be applied specifically to the security of electronic files and systems in libraries?

LIBRARY-SPECIFIC CONCERNS

Besides the generic concerns associated with securing electronic files or systems, there are four broad areas of library-specific concerns. These are diversity of databases, database privacy, ease of use, and the need to secure. The latter topic introduces risk analysis as a means to study security of electronics in libraries.

DIVERSITY OF DATABASES

Library databases cover a broad spectrum of configurations. Small libraries or elementary school libraries may have unique or singly purchased electronic databases on stand-alone platforms. Special libraries, especially corporate libraries, may be able to offer very sophisticated internationally linked databases. Academic libraries may fall anywhere between, depending on the size of the budget and the institution's commitment to expanding the scope of the traditional book budget.

Bibliographic Databases

Obviously, and increasingly, databases are bibliographic. Bibliographic databases may include individual library catalogs or bibliographic records from other institutions, such as regional or statewide union catalogs. Bibliographic databases may also include those of network consortia, such as OCLC and its regional nodes. Organizational entities that provide access to bibliographic databases at regional and state levels include MELVYL (the University of California's online catalog), NAAL (the Network of Alabama Academic Libraries), RLG (Research Libraries Group), CCLA (the College Center for Library Automation), TRLN (the Triangle Research Libraries Network), ILLINET (the Illinois Library and Information Network), OhioLink, and the CARL Corporation.

Electronic Information Sources

Commercial electronic information sources can be loaded on local networks. Such sources include electronic files provided by Project Muse, DIALOG, and the Government Printing Office. State or regional consortia, like Georgia's GALILEO Project, purchase files to make them available to their members. Occasionally, some electronic information sources are still found on stand-alone CD-ROM stations. Examples of these may be telephone books or college catalogs.

Patron and Related Parent Databases

Libraries maintain patron records and a variety of other institutional or parent records about borrowers. For example, patron records may come from county voter registration files or from a central student database. These records, from multiple sources, are locally massaged and stored in a format appropriate for the library's services. To maintain file integrity, central parent files may need to be interrogated and updated or corrected. For example, if a borrower's address changes, the library's record must be changed so that notices can be sent to the correct address. Also, the parent agency may need to be notified of the change. In university settings, for example, borrowers who exceed a variety of defaults (such as a limit on the number of items currently borrowed, a maximum amount of unpaid fines or fees, or an expiration on borrowing privileges) may be blocked not only from further borrowing but also from registration for the ensuing term. When the library account is cleared, the registration system must be notified. Consequently the flow of data between the library file and the registration file may need to be bidirectional. Such cooperation, however, further expands the risks for security breaches.

Financial Records

Generally, financial records must meet the strict requirements of an internal auditing group. Financial records include budgets, acquisitions records, collection development expenditures and balance files, cash receipt files from photocopying centers or circulation desks, and other records related to budgeting, encumbering, and spending. Loss of these records could be nearly catastrophic for a library. Security systems that do not prohibit tampering with these records are useless.

Vendor Records

Vendor records are most often associated with systems for acquisitions and collection development. They may also be useful for administrative purposes. Additionally, matrix information for serials check-in and claiming may be a part of vendor records. Electronic Data Interchange (EDI) is increasingly popular for ordering materials directly from jobbers. EDI records are complex. Security must be a high priority, as both account numbers and budgetary information are transferred electronically. These transfers are also bidirectional.

Personnel and Other Management Records

Management records such as payroll, budget, annual reports, proposals, and items requiring timing all need to be secure. The latter category could include such records as notifications triggered by the anniversary date of employment, the promotion and tenure timelines for library faculty, or salary and medical records for employees. In an automated environment, system set-up, log-in protocols, passwords, and operations information may also be maintained online. Frequently paper copies are not created for these files because the presence of a paper file may inhibit the flexibility to make needed spur-of-the-moment changes. In one medium-sized academic library, the matrix for the circulation system filled 6,000 cells. This document was 55 pages long when printed. After the first printing, it was backed up on disk but maintained in an electronic file.

DATABASE PRIVACY

Privacy and confidentiality of records are key elements in any system. When digitally stored, records also must be carefully secured. In libraries, digitized information may relate to patrons, management records, confidential files, or personal mail and files. Shared access, such as in a LAN (Local Area Network) or intranet environment, increases security vulnerabilities.

Patron Records

In many states, laws protect records about patrons and their borrowing habits. That means, unless subpoenaed, library personnel cannot reveal information about users. How libraries assure this level of privacy is a challenge. For example, when books are discharged from the circulation system, one library drops all information about the previous borrower. No history file is maintained on the items the person has borrowed. Neither does historical borrower information appear in the item record. This arrangement reduces the temptation for someone to reveal, with malicious intent or by accident, information about a previous borrower. At the same time, it eliminates the possibility that staff could review an item record and discover who, for example, had damaged a particular book. While selected statistical features were disabled by this management decision, the security of the records remained a high priority.

Libraries may need written policies regarding what level of employees may have access to borrower records and personal information from the patron record. These policies may be supported by password protection or by limiting access to certain employees. In the sophisticated electronic world, systems security must also include protocol for revealing borrower information over the telephone and at service desks. With a distributed system, policies must be understood and applied in a consistent way.

Management Records

All personnel records must be secured. Some states have enacted "sunshine laws" that allow access to select personnel records on demand. These records remain private until the appropriate legal conditions are met for access. Usually these conditions include a paper file of authorizations. Decisions need to be made about accepting formal papers that require a signature, via e-mail or fax.

Confidential Files

Confidential files include bid records, personnel evaluations, student academic records, reorganization plans, proposals, and other planning documents. Often this information should not be revealed until an appropriate date. Revealing bid files to incorrect people or at the wrong time, for example, could undermine an entire project. Inappropriate release of student records could violate confidentiality and increase the risk of a lawsuit. Further, issues of copyright protection and the application of licensing agreements for commercial sources must be resolved.

Personal Mail and Files

Increasingly, library employees are writing and receiving correspondence electronically. Files of drafts and final documents are also being stored electronically. Ever more professional committee work is being completed through the Web and various e-mail systems. These files also must be protected. Finally, decisions must be made about how much personal use of the Web and e-mail services will be tolerated and how it will be tracked. If attention is paid to this topic, some legal protection may be required to permit the institution to act if an employee makes inappropriate use of computer time.

EASE OF USE

Security protection should not interfere with either the ease of use or the user friendliness of the systems. One core value of libraries today is access. We pride ourselves on creating friendly staff, willing and eager to help all coming through our doors. We are largely successful at that goal, too! Our public electronic systems should reflect this value. Workroom and office computing may need a different standard. Greater security should be required for staff performing various automated functions.

NEED TO SECURE

With the coming of the virtual library, our doors are bigger and wider than ever before. The virtual library has expanded our traditional service area. E-mail and access to massive bibliographic and informational databases also have expanded our traditional service area. With this expansion comes an increase in use of library systems by persons who may not fit the old model of our service area. This increase in users also increases the security vulnerabilities. Licensing agreements need to be considered as we look at how to serve our various constituents. (Bielefield and Cheeseman, 1999: 24–27)

One basic tenet of computing security relates to the need to secure. The Principle of Adequate Protection states: "Computer items must be protected only until they lose their value. They must be protected to a degree consistent with their value." (Pfleeger, 1997: 9) Is there really a need to secure something? Yes, hardware and software need to be protected. Is it still necessary to protect the data? If the file consists of old information, is it necessary to expend energy protecting it? Many models for securing a variety of computing environments are presented in the literature of the computing field. (Rubin, Geer, and Ranum, 1997; Summers, 1997; Salter et al., 1998: 3–6; Krause and Tipton, 1999) These models and their underlying theories are outside the scope of this chapter. However, the remainder of this chapter presents some practical information on how to create a security program for a variety of computer components in a library environment.

LIBRARY-SPECIFIC SOLUTIONS

The interplay between the fundamental goals of computing security (confidentiality, integrity, and availability) and the vulnerabilities of computer systems (hardware, software, and data) creates a plethora of opportunities to design a security program for any library. Similar to the security analyses that were done for the general collection and for the safety of users and staff, the development of a security program for a library's electronic files and systems involves a risk management process. Once the risk management process is detailed, the chapter concludes with mention of ethics, policies, procedures, and legal issues impacting libraries.

THE RISK MANAGEMENT PROCESS

Risk management is a probability-based process that answers the following types of questions:

- What are our computing assets?
- What do we need to know about these assets?
- How are they stored and maintained?
- What about supplies and replacement parts?
- What are our risks? What could go wrong?
- What would be the impact of this?
- How often could it happen?
- What can be done?
- How much will it cost?
- Is it worth it?

A traditional risk management process has three aspects—performing a risk analysis, providing a risk assessment, and creating the final risk management plan. Depending on the size of the library, a formal risk management process may be more time-consuming than is necessary for protecting a small number of assets.

Completing an extensive risk analysis is the first formal step in an overall plan to design security for a library's computing environment. In most libraries, a risk analysis should be an item-by-item enumeration of what is available, where it is located, and how it relates to other items. Although specific disaster recovery procedures are outside the scope of this chapter, the results of a risk analysis of assets could also be critical for insurance purposes and for recovery in case of a disaster.

A risk analysis is a basic way to detail all the assets of the library's computing environment. However, its real purpose is to create an assessment of possible risks or vulnerabilities. Using the assessment, libraries can make informed decisions about safeguards for their own computing elements. Risk assessment can lead to a decision that current safeguards are adequate or to decisions to design specific additional safeguards. Together, risk analysis and assessment "effectively calculate the chance of experiencing the undesirable outcome, as well as its magnitude." (Ozier, 1999: 425) The risk assessment process identifies and documents the vulnerabilities for each item category named in the risk analysis. The risk assessment also suggests the likelihood of occurrence for each of the potential vulnerabilities against each type of named asset. If safeguards are already in place for items named in the analysis, these measures will be included as a part of the assessment also. Considering what could go wrong and the likelihood of that happening is a process that always provides a basis for action. That action is called the risk management plan.

The final phase of the risk management process is the creation of such a comprehensive risk management plan. Included in this plan would be "methods of protection, prevention, detection, and recovery." (Benson, 1998: 8) The formal plan should also include mention of expected annual losses, and a survey of suggested safeguards and their projected costs. A final recommendation for safeguards should mention the projected annual savings of each suggested safeguard. While this latter part of the plan may be more extensive than most libraries need, there are a variety of formulas designed to help in the compilation of cost savings. (Buck, 1991: 62–66; Summers, 1997: 6–7) Elements of a risk management program are detailed in the following sections.

Name and Label Hardware and Peripherals

A risk analysis can be performed on all pieces of hardware and peripherals by using an inventory format. The process should begin with naming and labeling each electronic workstation, server, peripheral, and storage device. A library-wide naming convention should be established. One generic naming convention is to name each item first by its department and then by a unique sequential number (for example, CAT-001). Objects with similar functions or locations should be numbered close together for ease in reporting problems. If the workstations at the circulation desk are all down, for example, a call that reports "CIRC-001 to CIRC-005" is easier than a call reporting a string of nonsequential numbers. If a department or unit has a series of workstations that all have the same elements (CPU, keyboard, monitor, mouse), each workstation could receive a group identification number. For example, a public service workstation could be numbered "PS-010." To request a repair, the staff member would have to specify the type of equipment plus the number. For example, "The monitor on PS-010 will not respond." A less-effective way to name equipment is with the name of the staff member currently assigned to the equipment. If that method is chosen, the equipment name must be changed every time the incumbent changes. After each piece of equipment is named, the name of the item should be attached to it in some recognizable way. Colored tape could be cut and applied to the item, for example. Permanent laundry markers could also be used. Labels that are easily removed or that fall off should be avoided. Everyone should know where the unit number is placed on each piece. That is, the identification numbers for monitors should always be in the same place on each monitor.

Design and Complete an Identification Log

Once the equipment is named and labeled, the second step of a risk analysis is designing and completing an identification log. A log form can be custom designed to address the unique identification, information, and insurance needs of the library. Such a log should be made for each named piece in the risk analysis. Logs can be organized by equipment type (keyboards), by department, or by some combination of the two. For each piece of equipment, all the pertinent information about that item should be recorded in the same way. Recording only one piece of equipment per log page is very important.

The completed logs should be stored electronically and in a printed notebook format, for easy reference in case the system goes down. If the library's configuration consists of many items or complex arrangements, both a disk of the file and a print copy of the log notebook should also be stored off-site. Categories within the log should be individualized for each library system. Format and spacing should be designed for ease of use and for clarity. Each item's log page may actually be longer than one physical sheet of paper. An example log page appears in Figure 4.1.

Create a Schematic Diagram

The third activity in a risk analysis involves creating a schematic diagram of the layout of the equipment within the entire library. This will also be a time-consuming and complex task. The pictorial representation for the schematic should show each individual piece of equipment and its label. Relationships between the various pieces of equipment, including their cabling, ought to be included in the diagram. Management software may be useful in creating the schematic. (Benson, 1998: 7–8) The final schematic should be stored in both the online and the print logs. A print copy also should be posted in a readily accessible place. It is usual to find such a diagram on the office wall of the library's automation specialist.

Figure 4.1: Sample Identification Log

IDENTIFICATION LOG
NAME OF LIBRARY

Type of Equipment: <u>CPU</u>   Unique ID Number: <u>PS-012</u>
Location: <u>Reserve Room</u>

Manufacturer:
Manufacturer's serial number:
Model type/Style/Size:
Institution's property code number:
Location of institution's property code number label:
Purchased or leased:
Date purchased or leased:
Date the lease expires:
Cost:
Vendor:
Vendor's address:
Vendor contact:
Vendor's phone/e-mail/fax:
Warranty information:
Service contract?
With whom?
Service contract phone/e-mail/fax:
Inclusive dates of service contracts:
Memory:
Speed:
Drives (describe):
    A:
    B:
    C:
    Other:
Modem line number, if appropriate:
Printer connection, if appropriate:
Peripherals, list with model information:
    -sound card
    -video adapter
    -network adapter
    -other
Date and Nature of repairs:
Special notes, including quirks:
Passwords:
Vulnerabilities (list):
Safeguards (list):

Designate Library Contacts

Next, a contact person should be appointed to represent each asset identified in the log. In large libraries more than one person may need to be appointed. These appointees might represent a department or a cluster of workstations. They should be intimately involved in the development and completion of the log of hardware and peripherals. Each designee must be trained in the nuances of the various systems under their auspices. Each ought to be trained for loading and updating various software systems as well. When a problem is detected, this person should be the first-line contact. If this person cannot resolve the problem, then the library's "computer person" must be called. The names of the contacts and their phone numbers should be included in the online and the print logs. Logs should be updated as staff responsibility changes. In small libraries, only one person may be in charge of all automation functions. If this is the case, a fully trained backup who can do all the same functions as the "computer person" is essential.

Gather and Store Documentation

Other assets, such as documentation, while not strictly a part of the computer system, are also essential to its smooth operation. The fifth step in the risk management process is to gather and store documentation. Documentation includes operating and troubleshooting manuals for programs, hardware, peripherals, individual systems, and the entire system in a large operation. Set-up instructions, administrative procedures, and warranty information all form a part of the library's computing documentation. Bar code or magnetic stripe information, attached to all new equipment or to software packages, represents another important part of the requisite documentation.

Documentation should be centrally stored within the library according to a specific retention plan. If possible, each department also should retain one copy of the documentation for each identified item type within that department. Depending on the organizational structure of the library's automation program, the appointed contact people ought to be responsible for maintaining representative documentation for their own areas of responsibility. An additional copy of all documentation should be stored off-site. All pieces of documentation should be recorded as a part of the identification log.

As an aside, in libraries where many identical pieces of equipment are used, documentation must be retained for both the on-site and the off-site storage facilities, for the department, and for the designated representative. Beyond that, extra pieces of documentation may be discarded.

Inventory Supplies

Supplies for the computer environment include paper, forms, print cartridges, toner, magnetic media, bulbs, and replacement or backup parts for hardware and peripherals. Such items should be maintained separately from regular library supplies. The purpose of separating computing supplies from the rest of the library's supplies is to be able to determine the actual cost of the library's computing processes. Knowing this information is especially important if cost-recovery programs are in place. Finally, while we do not like to think of theft of computer supplies by employees, it is a possibility. Having a clear accounting of the supplies helps control the flow of supplies to the appropriate areas while also providing security to them.

In smaller libraries, supply storage may have to be centralized. If that is the case, the management file showing the ownership and use of the supplies needs to be very detailed. Risks to the supplies are increased. For example, theft and "borrowing" supplies are common occurrences when supplies are merged. Such risks need to be noted as a part of the assessment. The final risk management plan for supplies probably should include the recommendation to identify a secure physical space for them.

Organize Computing and Storage Facilities

A central and safe on-site place for managing the computing function for the library must be identified and stocked. This facility will be under the aegis of the library's computer specialist. Included in this area would be servers, files, and the management tools necessary to support the library's computing capabilities. In large libraries, the computer specialist and staff will be housed here as well.

This facility also will serve as the central storage site for all documentation about each type of hardware and peripheral that is a part of the library's computing environment. Ideally, computer-related supplies and replacement or backup parts will be housed here, too. Appropriate climate controls and a backup power supply must be an integral aspect of this location. Key control systems and restricted access may need to be considered.

Finally, a secure off-site storage facility is an important part of security for the electronic environment. Off-site storage facilities should be accessible and meet climate, power, and privacy standards. In cities with multiple libraries, each could provide off-site storage for another to reduce storage costs for all. Other creative arrangements could be made with local businesses or nonprofit organizations within the community.

The presence of storage areas introduces elements of risk. Physical access, hours of access, and the right to access must be arranged and monitored. Procedures are needed to control the ebb and flow of supplies, hardware, and peripherals—particularly since faulty light pens, keyboards, and mouses are so easily swapped for new ones that a security protocol dealing with their removal from the storage area may sometimes seem antithetical to service concerns. For off-site storage facilities, especially those obtained in kind, access by the owning agency must be contractually guided. Generally, such access is limited by separate keying and by agreements to limit access to times when the space borrower is present. Limiting key access, however, may violate fire code restrictions in certain jurisdictions. While the vulnerability of the contents of the off-site storage area may be high, the cost of protecting it beyond those costs already absorbed by the space's owner may be impractical and unreasonable. Many demands could generate ill will. Two choices are available to resolve these concerns. First, the risk management plan should note the vulnerabilities and explain the reasons for not increasing security. Second, the risk management plan should recommend that a more secure (and possibly more costly) facility be located.

Protect Software

Software includes a variety of programs, including source and object codes, commercial programs, home-designed programs, utility programs, operating systems, compilers, maintenance programs, applications, and diagnostics. For larger libraries, software that is related to the network environment might also need protection. Copies of software must be stored on- and off-site. Just as with documentation, one copy of each software package or module should also be stored within each department that uses it. If the library's designated computer person serves a specific area rather than a department, that person should also have a copy of the software. For networked operations, however, it is probably impossible and impractical to have multiple copies of network files available in the departments.

The risk analysis activity for software can employ a variety of automated management programs. (Summers, 1997: 624–633) Software management programs can be cursory or complex. The size of the computing operation for the library will determine the appropriate complexities of the selected software management programs. Most libraries cannot spend the thousands of dollars necessary to purchase a state-of-the-art software management program. Therefore, simple enumeration and recording in the identification log may be the most appropriate way to assess software security. Software introduced by users creates a large security risk because it cannot be logged. The risk management plan should indicate safeguards for prohibiting user introduction of software.

Internal protection of software, network security, telecommunications applications, antivirus protection, encryption techniques, authentication, and other technical programming solutions are also outside the scope of this chapter. Books, articles, manuals, and Internet browsing will all yield information about the internal protection of software. In addition, basic detailed specifics for beginners and pros can be found in many places. (Benson, 1998; Summers, 1997) All but the most basic information is quickly dated, but many theories undergird the realities of internal protection.

Guard Data

Data may be stored in magnetic or print format. Executable files, shared files, archival information, logs, and audit records comprise data. Analyzing risks to data is difficult because the value of each specific type of data may vary dramatically over a short period. As well, individual users may hold data of unknown origin. Personal data files will be the hardest to inventory; they are also the types of data that introduce the most risk. It is very important that individually held data be controlled and recorded. Relevant data files should be entered on the identification log. Users should be prohibited from loading personal data files and specific safeguards should assure that users cannot load personal files—they represent very high risks for the library's equipment. Data that are no longer relevant should be discarded. Print data may need to be shredded before being discarded.

Consider Users

Some risk analyses also delineate users as a unique element of their risk analysis inventory. If users are to be considered separately, all types of user categories should be mentioned in the risk analysis. For example, the library's mission statement might name several communities to be served. In public libraries, these groups could be called children, young adults, adults, and seniors. Other such communities might also be identified. If the library is engaged in a literacy program, for example, the participants in that program might be named as a separate community for purposes of delineating appropriate services. If this type of identification scheme is used, each community's name might represent the way its users are identified in the risk analysis document.

Each user community brings different needs and skills to the computing environment. Protection needs in a public area may be different from protection needs in an office. The incorrect use of systems and software may need to be considered separately when users are identified as their own risk category. The threat of hacking and challenges to licensing agreements present other serious concerns. When users are considered in the risk analysis, staff, patrons, and administrators must be included.

Plan for the Portable-Computing Environment

In some cases, the components of the portable-computing environment are considered a separate part of the risk analysis process. If the library does use this area as a separate category, then password protection, authentication, dial-up protocol, access to servers, access to licensed information, and the like must be assessed. Risks are much greater and the risk management program to be developed must be more complex when a portable-computing environment is treated as a separate entity. Alternatively, regarding the elements of the portable-computing environment as a routine part of the library's overall environment is also appropriate. When this approach is used, the unique elements of portability can be absorbed into the overall assessment of risks.

An example of a chart that could be used as a model for a risk assessment program appears in Figure 4.2. Obviously, a real risk management plan will contain many pages and a lot more detail than shown

Figure 4.2: Sample Risk Management Plan					
RISK MANAGEMENT PLAN—SUMMARY—DATE					
TYPE	#	COST EA.	VALUE TOTAL	VULNERABILITIES	SAFEGUARDS
Hardware Monitors Brand A Brand B	12 .	$500.00 .	$6000.00 .	-PUBLIC- Theft Spills Vandalism -OFFICE-	 Cables No food policy Observation
Software Network Applications DocWeed	 1	 $500.00	 $500.00	Office use only Loss Outdating	Loaded on hard drive, backup in storage Subscription
Data Commercial Personal Payroll					
Storage					

Figure 4.3: Sample Corporate Security Policy

Computing in the—NAME OF LIBRARY—is designed to support the academic objectives of the college. It will reflect the current mission statement and the specific strategic plans of this library.

---

in this example. Most basic computer security books also suggest a variety of ways a risk management plan can be presented.

POLICIES AND PROCEDURES

Policies are written to support the mission and the strategic goals of the library. Policies supporting the security of electronic files and services are no exception. They undergird all aspects of the library's computing environment. Procedures are those applications that are in place to support the policies.

Policies

Not surprisingly, computing professionals have identified three types of policies. The first type is the "corporate security policy." By this is meant "the set of laws, rules, and practices that regulate how assets including sensitive information are managed, protected, and distributed within a user organization." (Summers, 1997: 568) The corporate security policy emanates from management. It is designed to reflect what the library and the parent organization are able to do or to support. For that reason, library computer specialists and others from the library staff should be involved in developing this policy. The corporate security policy is the umbrella policy for the library's computing environment. Such policies can be very brief, as shown in Figure 4.3.

Of course, the corporate security policy can take many forms. It can be significantly more detailed than the above statement. The University of Pennsylvania, for example, identified priority levels for use of the library. These levels ranged from the highest priority to the lowest and included what is forbidden. (Smith, 1999: 17–18) For libraries that have placed the needs of their various user communities into tiers, this approach is also excellent. Both the layout of the corporate security policy and its contents can vary according to the needs of the library and its parent institution.

The second type of security policy is called the "system security policy." (Summers, 1997: 568) It creates a policy for each specific computing system. While there will be only one corporate security policy, there will be individual policies for each system in the library. For example, if a public library's mission is to support entertainment and recreational use, then the Internet policy for that library might allow access to e-mail and chat rooms. (Smith, 1999: 23) In that case, this

---

Figure 4.4: Sample Inclusive System Security Policy Statement

The—NAME OF LIBRARY—supports free access to the Internet, including e-mail and chat rooms.

---

library's Internet system policy statement might resemble that shown in Figure 4.4. If, on the other hand, a college library is offering fee-based information retrieval services, their policy for community use of Dialog is probably restricted by the licensing agreement. In that case their policy might resemble that shown in Figure 4.5.

The Information Technology Security Evaluation Criteria identify the third type of security policy as the "technical security policy." That is "the set of laws, rules, and practices regulating the processing of sensitive information and the use of resources by the hardware and software of an IT [information technology] system or product." (Summers, 1997: 568) A library could have many technical security policies. For example, if a library restricts loading software onto a system until it has been tested and approved by the computer specialist, one of its technical security policies might read as shown in Figure 4.6.

The library also will have technical policies relating to internal management of the system. These policies will include "details on passwords, access levels, physical security, Internet threats, viruses, and response." (Blacharski, 1998: 371) Systems and technical security policies for libraries will answer many questions. Even more questions are raised when the systems are to be used in public areas. Among the questions that may be answered by such policies are:

- Who may use the computers?
- What software may they use?
- May they load personal data?
- Who may use the printers?
- Is there a time limit on computers?
- Will there be filtering?
- Will workstations be purchased to support accommodations

Figure 4.5: Sample Exclusive System Security Policy Statement

Use of the Dialog system in—NAME OF LIBRARY—is restricted to students, faculty, and staff of the college.

Figure 4.6: Sample Technical Security Policy

Employees of—NAME OF LIBRARY—must receive written permission before loading software onto library systems.

---

provided by ADA (Americans with Disabilities Act)?
- Will Internet use be offered? How?
- May catalog data be downloaded?
- What about consortium agreements?
- What happens when the systems go down?

An array of policies can be developed to support these and many other questions. However, acceptable-use policies must spell out explicitly what will be tolerated or supported. Policies should reflect the tenor of the community, the mission statement of the library, and the capabilities that can be supported by the systems, hardware, available staff, and the budget. They should be reviewed by legal representatives and should be enforceable. (Thomsen, 1999: 242)

Figure 4.7: Sample Policy Standard Statement

Librarians at the service desk will verify college affiliation prior to permitting use of a workstation.

Procedures

Procedures are detailed statements of how the various policies will be supported. In some cases, procedures evolve over time to reflect new information, to recognize reality-based experience, or to accommodate new service delivery methods. While the policies of the library will probably be published in some public way, the procedures usually are internal documents.

Benson includes "standards" as a point between policies and procedures. He describes standards as "shall" and "will" statements. (Benson, 1998: 30) For example, if a policy statement indicates the online catalog is restricted to students, faculty, and staff of a college, one standard for this policy might be stated as shown in Figure 4.7. A supporting procedure statement for this standard would be a detailed, step-by-step statement of how this verification process is to be completed. For example:

- Access to the workstation area is protected.
- Librarians at public service desks check for valid and current college ID cards.
- Librarians interrogate the online campus database to be sure the bearer of the card is a user in good standing. The steps for doing this are:
    1.
    2.
- If the person is a user in good standing, the librarian may admit that person to the workstation area.
- If the person is a library user who is not in good standing, the librarian may not admit the person to the workstation area.
- Admission to the area is by a key that is stored in the reference desk.

Procedures should be understandable, enforceable, and clearly stated. They should also reflect the laws of the jurisdiction in which the library is located.

ETHICS AND LEGAL ISSUES

Ethics and legalities are two sides of the same coin. Ethics refer to personal behavioral choices. In the computing environment, ethics generally refer to people or systems. Laws, on the other hand, are legislated behaviors and the tools for their enforcement.

Ethics

Ethics in the computing environment are intrinsically no different from other types of ethical issues. The applications are different, however. Library-related ethical issues can include:

- Copying proprietary software for one's own use
- Using library systems for personal use on library work time
- Failing to give proper copyright credit
- Using e-mail and other Internet applications for illegal purposes
- Sharing passwords and access codes to permit some activity that is not otherwise possible for a given user group

Short of posting library policies at workstations, there is not much an individual library can do to assure that users of public workstations are behaving in an ethical way. In some cases, if an egregious ethical violation occurs, it can be tracked. Most ethical violations occur out of sight. Public workstations that are in less-traveled areas should be protected by systemically permitting fewer functions. For

---

**Figure 4.8: Sample Policy and Standards Agreement
Statement**

I have read the policies and standards regarding computing in the—NAME
OF LIBRARY. I understand the policies and agree to abide by them. I further
understand that my employment may be terminated if I violate any of these
policies or standards.

---

example, those workstations might provide access to the local catalog
but not to the Internet.

Employers can take several actions to encourage ethical behavior
vis-à-vis the library's systems. One of the easiest solutions occurs on
the first day of work. New staff should be given a packet that contains a copy of the library's policies and standards regarding computers in the library. Staff should be given time to read these documents.
The last page of the packet should be a sheet indicating that the document has been read. That sheet should be signed and stored in the
staff member's personnel file. Staff should also be given a personal
copy of the packet and a copy of their signed statement. Just above
the signature line, a statement similar to the one shown in Figure 4.8
could be printed.

All staff must regularly reread the packet of policies and standards.
A good time to do this might be in conjunction with the annual performance evaluation. With each annual reading, the statement will be
signed indicating that the staff member still understands the library's
policies and standards and still agrees to adhere to them.

Likewise, policies and standards must treat users ethically. Privacy
must be assured, license agreements must be upheld consistently, and
contractual agreements must be fulfilled. Systems must be available
when they are promised, and they must perform as promised. If the
library is committed to an automated environment, all must be done
to assure availability of information—in some format.

Legal Issues

Much of what is written on laws and computers pertains to protection of government data, commercial data, and financial transactions.
These laws are revised as technology changes. Existing laws and statutes already deal with issues of privacy, secrecy, physical property, sabotage, extortion, embezzlement, terrorism, copyright, patents, and trade
secrets. These existing laws protect the computer environment to a
certain degree. They are also being updated to accommodate the computing environment. In addition, new state and federal laws are also

being written to address issues as they arise. Among the recent laws pertaining to computing are those on:

- Access
- Misuse of information
- Child pornography
- Theft of services
- Denial of services
- Computer fraud
- Viruses (Welch, 1999: 535)

Policies for computer use cannot be established if they violate laws of the jurisdiction in which the library resides. Procedures should indicate the enforcement protocol the library plans to use. Legal officials for the library/parent institution must approve all procedures.

SUMMARY

Many writers and systems engineers agree that complexity and security are antithetical. (Rubin, Geer, and Ranum, 1997: x; Barclay, 2000: 115) In this chapter, security of data and files has been discussed rather academically. In the first part of the chapter, objectives of confidentiality, integrity, and availability were explained. Vulnerabilities to the computing environment were identified as software, hardware, and data. Some generic safeguards were discussed as well. In the second part of the chapter, the library-specific concerns of database diversity, database privacy, ease of use, and the need to secure were identified. The risk management process was introduced as a way to identify the computing assets of the library. The chapter concluded with a brief discussion of policies, procedures, ethics, and legalities related to security in the library-computing environment.

The topic of computer security is huge. Many professional associations are engaged in identifying and studying issues of computer security. Theories abound. Internal solutions, such as encryption, are fun to read about but will probably be left to the systems personnel in the library or its parent institution. External solutions to physical security, such as cables and alarm systems for hardware, are discussed thoroughly in other sources. (Benson, 1998; Barclay, 2000: 117–121) The crucial point for electronic security is that some level of security for hardware, software, and data must be present. Generally, controls for such security can be achieved when applied at the levels of "data, programs, the system, physical devices, communications links, the environment, and personnel." (Pfleeger, 1997: 18)

Securing the library's computing environment is a holistic process. Each asset, vulnerability, and safeguard has a relationship with the other. Actions and reactions impact each other and the system as a whole. The challenge, then, is to find the right balance of protection and access to accomplish the library's mission.

REFERENCES

Barclay, Donald A. 2000. *Managing Public Access Computers: A How-To-Do-It Manual for Librarians*. New York: Neal-Schuman.

Benson, Allen C. 1998. *Securing PCs and Data in Libraries and Schools: A Handbook with Menuing, Anti-Virus, and Other Protective Software*. New York: Neal-Schuman.

Bielefield, Arlene, and Lawrence Cheeseman. 1999. *Interpreting and Negotiating Licensing Agreements: A Guidebook for the Library, Research, and Teaching Professions*. New York: Neal-Schuman.

Blacharski, Dan. 1998. *Network Security in a Mixed Environment*. Foster City, Calif.: IDG Books Worldwide.

Buck, Edward R., III. 1991. *Introduction to Data Security and Controls*. 2d ed. Boston: QED Technical Publishing Group.

Kou, Weidong. 1997. *Networking Security and Standards*. Boston: Kluwer Academic Publishers.

Krause, Micki, and Harold F. Tipton, eds. 1999. *Handbook of Information Security Management, 1999*. Boca Raton, Fla.: Auerbach.

Maier, Phillip Q. 1999. "Protecting the Portable Computing Environment." In *Handbook of Information Security Management, 1999*, edited by Micki Krause and Harold F. Tipton. Boca Raton, Fla.: Auerbach.

Ozier, Will. 1999. "Risk Analysis and Assessment." In *Handbook of Information Security Management, 1999*, edited by Micki Krause and Harold F. Tipton. Boca Raton, Fla.: Auerbach.

Pfleeger, Charles P. 1997. *Security in Computing*. 2d ed. Upper Saddle River, N.J.: Prentice-Hall.

Rubin, Aviel G., Daniel Geer, and Marcus J. Ranum. 1997. *Web Security Sourcebook*. New York: John Wiley & Sons.

Salter, Chris, O. Sami Saydjari, Bruce Schneier, and Jim Wallner. 1998. "Toward a Secure System Engineering Methodology." In *New Security Paradigms Workshop, Proceedings, September 22–25, 1998*. Charlottesville, Va.: ACM Press.

Smith, Mark. 1999. *Neal-Schuman Internet Policy Handbook for Libraries*. New York: Neal-Schuman.

Summers, Rita C. 1997. *Secure Computing: Threats and Safeguards*. New York: McGraw-Hill.

Thomsen, Elizabeth. 1999. *Rethinking Reference: The Reference Librarian's Practical Guide for Surviving Constant Change*. New York: Neal-Schuman.

Welch, Thomas. 1999. "Computer Crime Investigation and Computer Forensics." In *Handbook of Information Security Management, 1999*, edited by Micki Krause and Harold F. Tipton. Boca Raton, Fla.: Auerbach.

5 SECURITY OF SPECIAL COLLECTIONS

PROBLEM DESCRIBED

The terms "special," "archival," and "rare" all refer to specific types of materials or collections so important to an individual library that they must be separated from a general location and given additional protection. Sometimes these items are irreplaceable. Sometimes they reflect the unique history of a region or a person. Perhaps they represent the output of a favorite local author. Items may be placed in special collections because of cost, binding, illustrations, a specific printing technique, or age. Occasionally a donor has given personal memorabilia as a condition of a bequest. Many factors contribute to the placement of materials in special collections.

Once a library has decided to have an area of special collections, however, several questions about security must be answered. Where will the area be located? Who will staff it? How will users have access to it? How much extra protection, if any, will the area need? Experts on managing special collections and security analysts agree on some fundamental problems inherent in the security of the special collections area. These problems include the variety of materials to store and protect, environmental concerns, the escalating value of the materials, the possible lack of internal controls, human threats, an increased awareness of holdings, and security of users and staff.

VARIETY OF FORMATS AND MATERIALS

The aspect of special collections that makes it the most exciting is also one reason that security to the area is so difficult. Inherent in the notion of special collections is a wide variety of formats and materials. Among the formats found in special collections may be antiquities, archival records, audiovisual materials, books, government documents, manuscripts, maps, newspaper files, photographs, prints, realia, and reports. Many of these formats require unique equipment for reading, hearing, or viewing. This equipment, plus locked cabinets to display realia, and other special storage and display paraphernalia should be located within the special collections area. Special collections must also have space to evaluate and process collections.

Sometimes the library's preservation function is housed in the archival area. Such a decision requires additional work space, specialized preservation equipment, and other types of security. A separate and safe reading room for researchers must be made available near the archival area. Further, if the special collections area is also the focal point for showcasing the library, space may need to be allocated for occasional meetings or receptions. This decision also creates the need for additional types of security. Finally, some special collections areas also include or monitor basic or elaborate exhibit areas. Such exhibits might blend rare materials with materials on loan from donors or from other parts of the collection. Rare, expensive, and archival materials in exhibits require additional handling for security.

ENVIRONMENTAL CONCERNS

Items housed in special collections also must be stored in ways that protect them from the aging process. Also, the storage process must do no harm to the items. Because of these two requirements, many different storage devices may be needed. For example, besides standard and folio-sized shelving, special collections may need refrigeration capabilities, special HVAC (heating, ventilation, air conditioning) units, separate power supplies, and environmental monitoring devices.

Typically the housing of the special collections material is a decision that may have already been made by the library or the parent institution. Little attention may have been given to the impact of the environment on these rare materials. Temperature, humidity, mold, insects, fungus, dust, pollutants, water, and natural disasters comprise some environmental concerns for special collections areas.

ESCALATING VALUE OF MATERIALS

Theft of materials stored in special collections areas may create a special sense of loss. The emotional impact of such thefts is heightened because we may perceive these items as a part of our heritage or our culture. Thus, the theft or damage to special collections items is felt as a personal loss. Beyond the emotional impact, a definite financial loss occurs, as well. Special collections materials are increasing in value because they are generally irreplaceable. Items are out of print, one of a kind, or very valuable. An enormous market exists for special materials, especially those that are difficult to trace back to the original, such as art plates. Even art plates from rare or expensive books bring top dollar. As with so many other things, the financial value of special collections material continues to appreciate.

LACK OF INTERNAL CONTROLS

Archives and special collections should have much more stringent internal controls than the rest of the library. Comprehensive policies and procedures, which govern use of the collections, should be in place. Lack of such internal controls, or the misapplication of them, creates windows for opportunistic thieves.

Special collections should not be browsing collections. In smaller libraries where little attention can probably be paid to special collections, items are sometimes housed in locked glass-fronted cabinets. In our eagerness to showcase our special collections, restrictions on their use might be too relaxed for the safety of the collection.

HUMAN THREATS

Human threats come in many forms, including researchers, staff, and committed thieves. Shuman (1999: 32–33) describes a variety of methods used to get and to steal from special collections. These methods include:

- Picking locks
- Stealing keys
- Erasing ownership stamps
- Creating fictitious library markings
- Applying bogus call number labels
- Befriending staff members who, it is hoped, will then relax their attention to policies
- Using Internet-accessible library floor plans
- Targeting particular collections
- Finding libraries in areas that are suffering police shortages

Threats may be purposeful or accidental, but the result could be the same—destruction or loss of important materials.

Researchers

Researchers are well aware of the value of the rare, archival, and special materials that provide the basis for their research. Most scholars so appreciate the availability of the protected information they would do no intentional harm to it. Some, however, with that same appreciation, will try to pilfer the materials for their own use or financial reward. Also, with no malicious intent, researchers may damage materials with errant pen or pencil marks, with rough photocopying, or with normal bodily oils deposited on very old paper. Researchers may also inadvertently pick up special materials when they reload their briefcases. Finally, the mishandling of realia may cause damage.

Staff

The four categories of staff from whom the special collections must be protected are the staff of the special collections area, the staff from other areas of the library, the custodial staff, and the police or night patrol staff. First, staff of the special collections area is in a unique position to damage or steal rare materials. Staff members have unfettered access to collections. Staff can move collections from the stacks to the worktables and to their own desks with relative ease and generally without causing much attention. They can remove items after hours or through nonpublic doorways.

Staff from other areas of the library may also have easy access to special materials. In fact, at any point in the processing stream, items are vulnerable to staff. Staff members may be the most difficult thieves to detect since such thieves are frequently also able to hide evidence. For example, in a small library housing expensive books in glass cabinets, circulation staff may be charged with opening the glass cases to retrieve books for appropriate borrowers. Occasionally these materials may be borrowed; in other cases, they may need to be used within the library. Regardless, circulation staff, in this model, has access to the keys to these cases. Also, if the preservation function is managed in the special collections area, blending general collection items with special items through the preservation process may create other opportunities for theft by eager staff members.

Custodians who clean at night also may have free access to the special areas. Even if they do not have access to the stacks or storage areas, they may have access to individual staff workstations or to the processing area. Custodial staff may not be able to distinguish something that is rare from something that is old. They may inadvertently discard an important old document that seems out of place within the room. Finally, police or nighttime building monitors may have access to these special areas. Security people, while hired to protect the library and its resources, could take advantage of their position of trust to commit crimes. While we hate to think of our own staff or the staff of the parent institution as capable of committing such crimes, they do occur.

Committed Thieves

Some malicious people target special collections. Hours of research go into their discovering where particular materials are found and then figuring out how to gain access to them. Sometimes the theft is ego driven, at other times the value of the item is the cause of the theft. Sometimes thieves share information about special collections and share in the spoils of the heist. Among the most famous library thieves are James R. Shinn, Stephan Blumberg, Charles Merrill Mount, Kevin P. Gildea, William March Witherell, Gervase Donald Cheshire, and Elizabeth and Robert Bradford Murphy. (Shuman, 1999: 38–43) Their cases make interesting reading but also serve as eye-openers for security of the collections.

INCREASED AWARENESS OF HOLDINGS

With increasing use of the Internet and other publicity efforts, awareness and use of a library's special holdings has increased. Administrators and donors support this new interest in their collections. Use of collections is encouraged. Publicity for the library is high. Some Web pages even include detailed floor plans. Such availability of information, however, makes it easier for people committed to theft of special collections materials to identify and create a plan for pilfering such items.

SECURITY OF USERS AND STAFF

The last problem in security of special collections is security of users and staff. Many special collections are physically isolated from the general library and have small staffs. Such realities give way to concerns for the safety and the security of both users and employees.

SOLUTIONS

Archives and special collections can be secured in many physical ways.

- Create a unique lockable space for the area. In this area would be security devices and special locks, alarms, or buzzers.
- Control admission.
- Limit the number of simultaneous users.
- Lock up briefcases, outerwear, and umbrellas at the entrance.
- Permit each user to have only a few sheets of paper, a pencil, or a laptop computer in the area. Laptop cases would not be permitted in the secured area.
- Require researchers to sign in and provide some photo identification. Such identification might be retained until the user is ready to exit the area.
- Employ a room monitor. This attendant would help the researcher locate specific items in an online or printed finding aid.
- Close stack areas. Employees would retrieve materials from the closed stack areas. Researchers would be limited in the number of items they could use at one time.
- Limit photocopying. A photocopy machine would not be available for public use. Attendants would make all copies, if copying would not damage the materials.
- Require researchers to sign out after the attendant verifies that all materials used have been returned in appropriate condition.

This idyllic environment is certainly not possible everywhere, but some security measures should always be considered by a special collections supervisor. Such measures include doing a security audit, developing comprehensive security and disaster recovery plans, and training. A basic familiarity with insurance requirements and laws must be a part of the solutions for problems of securing special collections.

SECURITY AUDIT

A security audit of special collections may have already been a part of the overall security audit conducted for the general collection. If an audit was not done then, or if a general collections security audit was not done at all, a security audit is the first step in developing a comprehensive security plan for the special collection. The security audit will highlight potential problem areas in the special collections area. The audit should include an inventory of the collection, a review of the blueprints for the special collections area, and a schematic diagram of wiring and ventilation systems. The details of a generic security audit are presented in Chapter 1.

SECURITY PLAN

Just as in other parts of the overall library security program, a written security plan should be developed for the special collections area. The plan should build on results of the security audit. It should be proactive. Finally, it should be couched in terms of relevant federal, state, local, and institutional laws, guidelines, policies, and procedures. The security plan should contain current policies, procedures, and information on personnel involved. Names, telephone numbers, e-mail addresses, and mailing addresses for relevant law enforcement officials and rare book dealers should also be maintained as a part of the plan. The plan should be reviewed periodically and kept up-to-date. Elements of a security plan for special collections include the security team, users, proof of ownership, and physical security.

Security Team

The special collections security plan should begin with the appointment of a security officer for the special collections area. Frequently this person is the head of the special collections area, the archivist, or a curator. Many writers suggest this person should also be the library security officer (LSO) for the entire library. For this chapter, though, the special collections security officer will not also have responsibility for the entire library. As an aside, it is recommended that two library-wide LSOs be appointed. Each would have distinct responsibilities and they would work closely together. In this model, the curator could serve as the special collections and disaster team head, while someone else could serve as the security officer for the remainder of the library. In large libraries, having one person in charge of both aspects of security would be an overwhelming task and could leave the curator with little time for the curatorial and managerial aspects of that job.

Formally designating someone as the LSO offers distinct procedural advantages, especially in academic libraries. Academic libraries should work in concert with the Rare Books and Manuscripts Section (RBMS) of the Association of College and Research Libraries (ACRL). The special collections security officer should submit information to that agency to get added to their list of LSO contacts. Membership on this list provides access to information about thefts from other special collections. Such membership also helps keep archivists alerted about interesting "sales" in the area. The list of members is forwarded by RBMS to the Antiquarian Booksellers Association of America. For protection of the archives, it is essential to be part of the national effort to stop the misuse of the nation's special collections.

No matter how the labor is divided, the security officer should appoint a small committee to help design policies and procedures for the area. The team should work with institutional and local law enforcement officials. Local rare book dealers and appraisers should also be contacted and introduced to the special collection. They should understand the focus of the collection, the nature of any attempted or successful thefts, and how to identify the library's markings. Plans should be developed that answer the questions of whom to call and what documentation will be needed in case of a problem. In small libraries, a team may not be possible. If that is the case, a security consultant should be employed to develop the plan.

Users

The category of users includes researchers and staff. Many suggestions for increasing security to the special collections area are low cost. A high benefit occurs from these suggestions:

- Work primarily from appointments.
- Require registration before admittance.
- Require photo identification.
- Retain identification until the user is finished.
- Have researchers sign the registration form and a copy of the rules and regulations governing use of materials in the area.
- Treat signed documents as a contract.
- Allow only paper, pencil, or a laptop computer into the public area.
- Restrict access to nonpublic areas.
- Limit the number of people in the public area at one time.
- Require requests for materials to be in writing.

- Maintain user registration, contract information, and request information indefinitely.
- Inspect belongings as users depart.
- Apply policies and procedures uniformly.

A high-cost suggestion is to provide constant supervision of users. While this measure might be difficult for small libraries, it can prove to be an excellent safeguard.

"Good reference service leads to a more secure archives program." (Trinkaus-Randall, 1998: 100) Good service provides focused research experiences and appropriate use of researchers' time. Because the researchers are being served in such a professional manner, they have no "ax to grind" and therefore are less likely to damage materials due to frustration. Quality, focused reference assistance also minimizes wear and tear on the archival materials.

Good service begins with good employees. Screening new employees, an essential part of any overall security plan, is especially important for special collections. Some relatively low-cost tips for the internal security of the special collections area include:

- Limit key distribution.
- Have employees return keys upon departure.
- Inspect staff belongings upon departure from the area.

Higher-cost solutions include:

- Conduct background checks prior to hiring.
- Bond special collections employees.
- Key valuable collections separately.
- Change locks as often as possible.

Chapter 3 provides more detailed information on the security of users and employees.

Proof of Ownership

The issue of marking special or archival materials is a tricky one. First, marking the materials may disfigure and therefore devalue them immediately. Embossing, punching, or perforating methods should not be used. (Patkus, 1998: 85) Second, any kind of marking on old paper may cause further deterioration of the paper. Any marking must be in an appropriate marker that would not cause such deterioration. Third, some materials cannot be marked in a visible way. In such cases, indelible markings might need to be employed to identify property. (Eberhart, 2000: 360–361)

RBMS has published guidelines for security of special items. This document has an appendix devoted to suggestions about marking materials. These include:

- Provide visible markings, in appropriate ink, placed in such a way that an attempt to remove the markings would obviously damage the material.
- Use supplemental invisible markings to aid in identification of stolen items.
- Assure that markings unequivocally identify the repository by name.
- Give special consideration to markings on medieval and renaissance manuscripts, incunabula and early printed books, leaf books, leaves, and maps.
- Mark all removable or discrete parts.
- Develop a consistent marking policy and procedures.
- Mark every item as it is received.
- Mark all holdings retrospectively.

RBMS also suggests noting, in the catalog record, any physical markings or anything else that is unique about each item. Such notes will make it easier to identify the item if it is stolen. Records of purchase, gift, and ownership should also be included in the catalog record for each item. These records and markings will be necessary for insurance and appraisal purposes. (Guidelines for the Security of Rare Book, Manuscript, and Other Special Collections, 1999: 746–748)

Physical Security

Physical security of the special collections is critical to their preservation. Yet, use of their contents is an important reason for maintaining the collections. Striking the appropriate balance between security and use should be the goal of each repository. Many suggestions to enhance the security of the physical collection and supporting areas have already been presented in this chapter. Others are listed below. Suggestions are divided into areas related to cost.

Some relatively low-cost suggestions include:

- Control access to keys and vaults.
- Change locks or remove key card users from systems when they announce their intention to resign, or concurrently with a termination conference, if the person's employment is being ended.
- Require attendants to do all photocopying and scanning for users, if such reproductive techniques are appropriate.
- Do not permit food, drinks, or smoking in the area.
- Orient chairs in the public area so that they face only the monitor.

- Do not permit boxes of materials to obstruct the monitor's view.
- Train monitors in appropriate visual surveillance and room scanning techniques.
- Develop a disaster plan.
- Practice disaster recovery techniques.

Mid-priced suggestions for security also include:

- Provide secure storage areas for briefcases, coats, and other paraphernalia the users might normally be carrying.
- Secure fire exits, to the extent it is possible.
- Design the reading area so it can be easily monitored with an unobstructed view.
- Purchase supplies to support the disaster plan.

Big-ticket security measures include:

- Install video surveillance equipment.
- Maintain a 24–hour monitoring service.
- Employ human security monitors.
- Install sophisticated alarm systems.
- Install secured HVAC systems.
- Install HVAC systems that meet preservation specifications for temperature and relative humidity control and fluctuations.
- Minimize exposure to light and ultraviolet radiation.
- Attend a disaster recovery workshop.

Physical solutions to security concerns can range from the inexpensive to the very expensive. In most cases, the size of the repository, its budget, and the nature of the materials to be protected will dictate the strategies selected for security of the special collections. General collection security matters are discussed in more detail in Chapter 2.

DISASTER AND RECOVERY PLAN

Guidelines must be developed for how to prepare for, deal with, respond to, and recover from a variety of disasters. Allen (1998: 3–4) sees disaster plans as containing two sections. The first section would include:

- Appointing the security officer
- Creating catalog records for items as soon as they are received
- Including special notes in the catalog record to aid in the identification of each item
- Conducting inventories—both regular and spot

- Implementing an ownership marking program for new and retrospective holdings
- Developing and retaining user registration and request records
- Creating plans for monitoring public and private areas of the repository
- Creating plans for physical security

The first part of the disaster plan should have information about insurance. Insurance is discussed later in this chapter. Theft, mutilation, and natural disasters are the most common types of disasters that require specific plans. Other kinds of calamities can also occur in the special collections area.

Theft and Mutilation

Theft and mutilation of materials from special collections really is a disaster. Often the theft or mutilation is not apparent until long after it occurs. "The resulting disaster from theft or mutilation may be as devastating as any natural disaster for an institution's collections and staff morale." (Allen, 1997: 29) When theft is discovered, RBMS recommends the following activities:

- Notify the special collections security officer.
- Work with police and legal counsel to determine a plan of action.
- Plan publicity strategy.
- Notify donors, trustees, insurers.
- Notify booksellers, dealers, auction houses, databases, and listservs (such as ACRL's RBMS for academic libraries, and the Antiquarian Booksellers Association of America headquarters).
- Publicize losses.
- Preserve the evidence site.
- Identify all witnesses and have them write independent reports of what they know about the incident.
- Compile an inventory of missing items, including photographs, if possible.
- Transfer similar items to a more secure area.
- Arrange for an appraisal of loss.
- Maintain a diary of activities related to the case.
- Prosecute to the fullest extent.
- Be prepared to go to court.
- Reevaluate the security plan. (Guidelines Regarding Thefts in Libraries, 1994)

Natural Disasters

Technically there are three types of disasters. Only the third type is truly a natural disaster. However, for this chapter, all three types will be considered natural disasters because they are outside the control of the special collections area.

The first type of disaster is a "small-scale disaster." Events that affect one floor of a building or just one department fit this category. A leaky window, overflowing plumbing, or rodent infestation might be considered small-scale disasters. A "large-scale disaster" is the second identified category. Fires or large water main breaks that could result in services being suspended for a day or two while recovery efforts take effect are examples of this type of disaster. Finally, a "wide-area disaster" affects a whole geographic region and is what is normally called a natural disaster. Included in this category are hurricanes, floods, earthquakes, or events that affect the infrastructure of the area. (Kahn, 1998: 42)

Three phases of activity form the core of the action plan for all three classes of disasters. (Kahn, 1998: 35) Phase one is the planning stage. Here are the things to do in Phase one:

- Appoint a disaster team and backups.
- Establish salvage priorities based on type of disaster and format of materials.
- Write plans for all three types of disasters, including plans for public relations.
- Train the teams.
- Assign specific responsibilities to team members so there is no duplication of effort.
- Train the rest of the staff, including repository, custodial, and enforcement staff.
- Contact contractors who might be employed to help in the event of a disaster—consider contractors outside the area for large-scale disasters.
- Practice the plan.

The second stage of the disaster process begins when a disaster actually occurs. Here are the things to do in Phase two:

- Gather the disaster teams.
- Implement the internal plan.
- Engage outside contractors.
- Determine if the special collections area should be closed during restoration and for how long.
- Begin public relations and networking efforts.

Finally, the third stage in the overall response plan is the recovery phase. Initially it may seem like there will never be a "light at the end of the tunnel," but it will occur. Here are the things to do in the final phase:

- Restore critical services
- Phase in restoration of remaining services
- Evaluate the plan and making adjustments to it as necessary
- Celebrate!

The National Institute for the Conservation of Cultural Property is an excellent source of information for what to do in a disaster situation. (Their address is 3299 K Street, N.W., Washington, D.C. 20007–4415.) Also, in 1998 the American Library Association published a manual on disaster planning. This manual includes a large array of checklists and sample forms. (Kahn, 1998: 77–107)

Other Calamities

Writers call a variety of events "disasters." In fact, such events as power and cell phone outages, collapsing stacks, computer crashes, birds that fly in the front door and circle the reference desk, and others are probably merely inconveniences. Insofar as possible, the disaster plan should also identify what to do for these events. For example, a telephone tree is a good way to inform people of problems when the electricity is out. A telephone tree is simple to design. A computer-based list is another excellent way to notify all employees who are connected. In large buildings, certain floors may be missing power while others still have it. Electronic announcements are not much help if they are sent to staff without the power.

While librarians and archivists cannot predict or plan for all types of calamities or inconveniences, some constants occur in the identification of such events and how to deal with them. Accidents and injury to users or employees, for example, call for prompt action. The disaster plan should address these concerns, as well. The following steps are important for dealing with a situation involving people:

- Call 911, if appropriate.
- Remain calm.
- Evacuate the area, if necessary.
- Sound an audible alarm, unless that will jeopardize others.
- Sound an inaudible alarm, unless that could inflame a situation.

The disaster planning process and many elements of the actual disaster plan presented here for special collections both have widespread applicability. In fact, the same disaster planning process and plans should be used for the remainder of the library and for the general collections. Since disaster planning frequently involves restoration of damaged materials, tradition has placed overall coordination responsibilities for disasters (and some calamities) under the aegis of the special collections group.

TRAINING

The key to any successful program is training. Staff should be thoroughly trained in all procedures related to security and disaster management. They should know their roles in the implementation of the various plans. Staff should also understand the reasons behind these programs. Some managers fear that if people understand the reasons behind the procedures, they will then circumvent the system more easily. It is better to have thoroughly informed staff who understand the policies and procedures than to fear that training staff will make them better thieves. Staff buy-in is essential to the smooth operation of the various plans. Besides, the committed thief can bypass any system.

The security officer should plan and execute the training. Consider the following when developing a procedure for training staff about special collections (and the variety of emergency programs they manage):

- Orientation sessions for new staff
- Training courses for existing staff
- Regular refresher courses
- Classes for nonarchival staff
- Exhibits showcasing the rules of the area
- Exhibits showing what can happen to materials if the rules are not enforced (Trinkaus-Randall, 1998: 110)

Users of the special collections area should be given some training in correct procedures for using the area. Usually, this training can be in the format of an informational handout. This handout should be presented to researchers before they are admitted to the public area. It should be discussed with them to assure they understand. Many archives also have the researchers sign a statement of understanding of the procedures as a condition of admittance to the area.

INSURANCE

The first step in obtaining appropriate insurance coverage for the special collections area is a risk analysis performed by professionals. Professional appraisals of the collections may also be necessary. To be approved for regular or disaster insurance, archives must be able to prove that:

- Ownership of items is indicated by visible and invisible markings and by detailed cataloging records that indicate special features of specific pieces
- Items are accessioned and recorded as soon as they enter the archive, instead of after they are processed
- There are few or no processing backlogs
- A program of regular and random inventories occurs
- The most precious items are inventoried frequently
- Security programs are in place and applied uniformly
- The special collections systems of internal control are appropriate, applied uniformly, and monitored
- Accurate use records are maintained
- Training for preparedness and recovery are ongoing processes
- Sound hiring practices are employed

For academic libraries, the Association of College and Research Libraries (ACRL), a division of the American Library Association, suggests using its standards for meeting minimal protective requirements. (Standards for Ethical Conduct, 1993) Insurers should be keenly aware of the contents of the collection and the recovery plans that are in place.

LAWS

In most of the areas discussed above, local legal requirements must always be addressed. These requirements may change from jurisdiction to jurisdiction. It is always wise to check all plans with the legal authority and the enforcement arm of the parent institution. Of particular concern to special collections should be those activities that:

- Require users to sign a form as a condition of admission to special collections areas. While such a form may be necessary for insurance purposes, it may not construe a legal contract.
- Retain request forms indefinitely. This retention, also important for insurance purposes, may violate the user's right to privacy.
- Claim the institution has a right to detain and check users' belongings as they exit the area. Other liabilities may befall the institution if it does not detain users for the purpose of checking their belongings.

Guidelines from both the ACRL and the Society of American Archivists encourage libraries and special collections to work with federal, state, and local legal officials to help in the development and execution of security plans for special collections. Chapter 7 addresses legal issues in more detail.

SUMMARY

ACRL's Rare Books and Manuscripts Section (RBMS) developed guidelines for securing special collections (Guidelines for the Security of Rare Book, Manuscript, and Other Special Collections, 1999). Their plan, much more detailed than this chapter, is also an excellent source for information. Trinkaus-Randall's (1995) manual on security for special collections is an excellent source for focused details on this specialized aspect of security. Additionally, ACRL's "Guidelines Regarding Thefts in Libraries" (1994) can be used with the RBMS document to add more detail and color to the planning process.

Despite all the hard work by the professional associations on behalf of security for special collections, Allen (1997: 37–38) notes that the attitude of the media can be a deterrent to the public's sentiment regarding theft and mutilation of special collections materials. She believes that increased legislation will make the public more aware of the problem and of its magnitude. Perhaps, if penalties are stiffer, thieves will think again before they attack another special collection. Unfortunately, the problematic attitude is not exclusive to the media. Even librarians, who should know better, try to capitalize on theft and mutilation as humor. Since they do so in the professional journals of librarianship, it is safe to assume that librarians of all stripes (authors, reference librarians, and editors) still do not understand the significance of the problem. (Wartenberg, 2000)

Throughout most of the history of librarianship, protecting collections and protecting special collections were synonymous. This equation is no longer true. As our culture has changed, threats to the whole library have increased. Now, protecting special collections is just one aspect of the overall security concerns for the library. There are some differences, however. This chapter has addressed these differences.

REFERENCES

Allen, Susan M. 1997. "Preventing Theft in Academic Libraries and Special Collections." *Library & Archival Security* 14, no. 1: 29–43.

———. 1998. "Theft in Libraries and Archives: What to Do During the Aftermath of a Theft." In *Management of Library and Archival Security: From the Outside Looking In*, edited by Robert K. O'Neill. New York: Haworth.

Eberhart, George M. 2000. *The Whole Library Handbook 3: Current Data, Professional Advice, and Curiosa About Libraries and Library Services*. Chicago: American Library Association.

"Guidelines for the Security of Rare Book, Manuscript, and Other Special Collections: The Final Version, Approved July 1999." 1999. *College & Research Libraries News* 60 (October): 741–748.

"Guidelines Regarding Thefts in Libraries." 1994. *College & Research Libraries News* 60, no. 9 (November): 641–646.

Kahn, Miriam B. 1998. *Disaster Response and Planning for Libraries*. Chicago: American Library Association.

Patkus, Beth L. 1998. "Collection Security: The Preservation Perspective." In *Management of Library and Archival Security: From the Outside Looking In*, edited by Robert K. O'Neill. New York: Haworth.

Shuman, Bruce A. 1999. *Library Security and Safety Handbook: Prevention, Policies, and Procedures*. Chicago: American Library Association.

"Standards for Ethical Conduct of Rare Book, Manuscript, and Special Collections Libraries and Librarians, with Guidelines for Institutional Practice in Support of the Standards." 1993. *College & Research Libraries News* 54 (April):

Trinkaus-Randall, Gregor. 1995. *Protecting Your Collections: A Manual of Archival Security*. Chicago: Society of American Archivists.

———. 1998. "Library and Archival Security: Policies and Procedures to Protect Holdings from Theft and Damage." In *Management of Library and Archival Security: From the Outside Looking In*, edited by Robert K. O'Neill. New York: Haworth.

Wartenberg, Paul. 2000. "The Pros and Cons of Squelching Library Theft." *American Libraries* 31, no. 2 (February): 48–49.

6 SECURITY FOR SPECIAL EVENTS

AN OVERVIEW OF PLANNING

Sometimes a commercial, cultural, or social event occurs near the library and impacts library services and security in ways that are very different from most other events. The impact may even be unimaginable. In these unexpected cases, the need for library security may take on unusual or unpredictable characteristics. Social or political demonstrations, civil unrest, expansive parades, community cultural celebrations, presidential visits, rock concerts, major sporting championships, and national political party conventions are a few examples of large events that might impact library services in unpredictable ways. In Atlanta, the 1996 Olympics and Para-Olympics provided such an opportunity. While most of us will never have the opportunity to plan for library safety and security during events of this magnitude and duration, very little exists in the literature about such planning.

Why is that the case? The main reason for this dearth of information is security. That is, the element of surprise is one factor in keeping people safe. For Atlanta libraries, the 1996 Olympics and Para-Olympics provided an opportunity to understand security in a new way. The information local institutions received on their role, the impact of traffic, and the expectations for the citizenry seemed to change from day to day, from meeting to meeting, and from one newspaper article to the next. There was a weekly ebb and flow of frustration as everyone tried to plan something (anything) in absence of real information from Olympic headquarters. It was not until the very last minute that librarians realized we were not in charge of planning security for our libraries. We were in charge only of reacting to security plans that had been made without our knowledge. That purposeful (and secretive) approach to security was the cornerstone of the overall security plan for that three-week period. The purpose of this chapter is to share some information on planning for safety and security in the presence of major events.

Planning is definitely the name of the game when a library has an opportunity to participate in something the size and scope of the Olympics. Two kinds of planning seemed to occur simultaneously. These were "planning by imaginative thinking and newspaper accounts" and "planning by reality check." Planning by imaginative thinking and newspaper accounts occurred each day when the local newspaper was read and a new pronouncement about what was "really" going to happen was printed. We would convene another meeting and plan for how we would provide services under the latest guideline. On the other hand, planning by reality check occurred when an official announcement was made—frequently at the last minute. These usually required a complete change in the plans previously made.

PLANNING BY IMAGINATIVE THINKING AND NEWSPAPER ACCOUNTS

It is hard to identify when library employees in the metropolitan Atlanta area realized the magnitude of security issues involved in hosting a special event such as the Olympics. When we first heard the Olympics were coming to Atlanta, the first things we thought about were exhibits, fun, and showcasing the city. Our first realization that security was foremost on the minds of the event planners came when several local librarians were scheduled to meet in Atlanta. It was an important meeting and the group from the Georgia Institute of Technology was very late. When they finally arrived, they declared that their campus had been sealed!

Georgia Tech was home of the Olympic Village—housing for the athletes, coaches, and trainers. The library was right in the middle of the sealed area. Tech librarians would work side-by-side with the athletes. Representatives to the meeting had previously told the group of the elaborate credentialing process required for all employees. All Georgia Tech employees knew the campus would be sealed to outsiders; however, they did not know the exact date the campus would be closed. They did not know, until they arrived at work that day, that on-campus parking would be unavailable until after both special events! On that day they were told to go home and return to campus via alternate means. (Frank et al., 1997)

Throughout the University System of Georgia, the summer schedule was tweaked in order not to have classes during this period. Many campuses throughout the state were either near or a part of Olympic venues. Georgia State University (GSU), in Atlanta, anticipated foot traffic tickling the edges of its sprawling urban campus. The university hoped to showcase itself with an eye toward recruiting students. It was a once-in-a-lifetime recruiting opportunity. To that end, the library's special collections department began planning for a major exhibit on women athletes. This exhibit would be housed in the administration building and would be enhanced by additional exhibits throughout the library.

The university-wide challenge at GSU was to provide easy access for visitors, an attractive facility to draw them in, and a work schedule that was flexible enough to allow staff to attend events. The library adopted those goals as its own. From the perspective of library security, the service goal for this period did not change—the library would remain open as much as possible. An excellent security program was already in place. An electronic book-theft-detection system, monitored by student assistants, had been successful for many years. The campus police made regular uniformed and plainclothes patrols of the building, and police emergency telephones were on each floor of the building. Classes would not be in session. Since average use of the building included about 7,000 entrants per day during a regular academic term, it seemed that regular security measures would suffice. Two public entrances/exits needed to be monitored; staff assumed they would continue to be able to find student assistant employees to monitor these doors.

PLANNING BY REALITY CHECK

Typically, the GSU library shortened service hours when classes were not in session. As time drew nigh, the public services staff became increasingly concerned about the consequences of trying to maintain either a regular or a traditional shortened schedule during the three-week period. The plan for showcasing the library and its exhibits called for maintaining a full range of service hours. While Georgia Tech would be serving the research needs of the athletes and their attendants, the GSU university library also had a research role. It would provide research assistance to the Olympics visitors, to its own constituencies whose research would continue, and (through a long-standing reciprocal agreement with Georgia Tech) to Georgia Tech students and faculty who would have no physical access to their own library.

However, the GSU library's own employees had obviously hoped to take off much time during these two major events. Many staff members were expecting out-of-town guests; many had purchased tickets to multiple events. Several employees had saved annual leave to take the entire time off; a handful of library employees was leaving town to get away from all the predicted confusion. Others were concerned about the traffic situation. Still others were concerned about security. Many student assistant employees had no intention of working while classes were not in session. The potential lack of staff became a huge concern. Reluctantly, the library's planning committee began to look at scaling back public hours and plans to showcase the library.

Soon, the city began issuing traffic advisories. Residents were urged not to plan to go downtown unless necessary. Businesses were asked to close or scale back hours. Everyone was being asked to increase personal use of public transportation to get into the central core. Concomitantly, the city predicted very heavy use of public transportation. People were warned to plan on delays of several hours' duration in the public transportation system. Staff began to fear four hours of commuting time on top of the regular eight-hour day. Concerned, the library's administration began asking staff to submit their preferred schedules for the entire Olympics period. As these requests appeared, it became obvious there would be scheduling concerns. Some staff wanted to maintain their regular schedules throughout, some wanted to be off, and others wanted to have the customary flexible time. All over campus, scheduling issues were being discussed as pressure mounted from the city to plan to reduce the traffic coming into the downtown area during the Olympics.

THE SECURITY PLAN

One day library employees noticed that the manholes near the library were being sealed. Employees were told this was a safety measure. Soon after, the library was told that, because of proximity to a sporting venue and because the library provided a direct sight line into the venue, the library would be closed to the public. The library was also told the campus police could not help secure the building. All officers would be providing enhanced security to the entire campus. At that point, plans for exhibits were scratched and the focus shifted to serious security for the building and its staff. The lessons learned are summarized in the following sections.

STEPS TO SECURE THE LIBRARY FOR MAJOR EVENTS

- Close the library to the public.
- Make special identification cards for all staff and prohibit access to the building for anyone without this identification. If anyone other than library staff needs to enter the building, have a special ID badge waiting for that person at the monitored entrance. Arrangements for such badges should be made through the library's administrative office.
- Close all entrances to the building except one.
- Change the locks for any other doors and only issue a few copies of the new keys. Have recipients sign for these new keys.
- Require all persons entering and exiting the building to sign in and out—even for breaks.
- Keep track of who is in the building. At the end of the day, if people cannot be found in the building, telephone them at home to see if they left the building without signing out.
- Control the hours the library is occupied. For example, allow staff to arrive at work as early as 6 A.M. and permit them to work only until 6 P.M. This rigidity allows for increased safety.
- Maintain daily work and vacation schedules of all staff. Arrange

these schedules in a readily accessible manner (perhaps in a note-book), and make that document available to anyone who needs to know if someone is scheduled to be at work.

- Rotate all available employees between the security points. Have some monitor the main entrance, manage the sign-in and sign-out procedure, and deny access to persons without special identification badges. Have others monitor the service entrance, assuring that no one enters that way.
- Provide cell phones at the monitoring points for emergencies or for informational reasons. Monitors can even use these phones at closing to call remaining staff members to remind them to leave on time.

SNIPPETS OF TRUTH
- The final plan can be very complicated.
- Library employees will be disappointed that the library cannot be showcased in any way.
- People really hate monitoring the doors.
- People feel vulnerable monitoring doors.
- Typically, even though the library is closed to the public, staff members who monitor the doors will not get as much of their own work done as they imagined.
- Several late workers could assist at closing to help their colleagues secure the building. These extra people speed up the closing process and enhance the monitor's sense of security.
- Micromanagement of schedules is not fun! People do not like having their schedules closely monitored.
- Part of the overall security for a major event is the element of surprise. While the library thinks it should be informed, the secrecy surrounding events is an integral part of the overall security plan.
- Cell phones can disappear during the night.
- Library users will have far fewer research needs than they imagined.
- Library employees can work together for a common goal.

SUMMARY

Library literature offers virtually nothing on the topic of security for such special events as major sporting events, major cultural events, or national political conventions. The literature in the field of arena management does deal with securing arenas during major events—the Super Bowl or national conventions of the major political parties, for example. However, arena literature is focused both on moving people about safely and on protecting the participants—athletes, musicians, and the like—and, unlike the Atlanta libraries during the Olympics, arena managers typically can use contracted security and local police forces.

At the University of South Florida (USF), a detailed special events security planning system is in place for the special events held on campus (Bromley, 1984). The system includes considerations of the purpose of the event, crowd size and composition, advertising, fees, crowd control provisions, rules and laws, traffic, and parking. Also, the history of the performers or the special events at other venues is also considered. Further, USF requires the involvement of campus security and legal advisors early in the planning stage.

TIPS

If a library is involved in something big that will affect the traffic patterns in and around the library, there are some planning tips to keep in mind:

- Begin early and envision a variety of plans.
- Plan for security of the facility; work with local police or campus security.
- Do not depend on local security or on contracted security firms to provide additional security.
- Reduce hours or close for the event.
- Limit access to the building to selected people and decide how they will be recognized. Important topics to consider are badges, sign-in and sign-out sheets, and monitoring.
- Work with human resources to plan how staff will be compensated for any missed work time. Legal issues may need to be considered.
- Decide who will manage the security function.
- Decide what kinds of schedules can be arranged. Can the library close entirely or close early one day? Can staff telecommute? Can special projects be completed at home? How will at-home time be granted? How will work completed at home be assessed? How can schedule flexibilities and other options be offered equitably?
- Overindulge schedule flexibility. Allow as much vacation and flexible time as possible.
- Everyone who wants to be off to attend a function should be able to do so.
- Plan for what will happen if someone compromises the security plan.

Although librarians do not often get the chance to participate in a planning process of this magnitude (thank goodness!), a lot of planning can make it fun. The most important fact to keep in mind is that the element of surprise is central to security planning. To manage the ever-changing environment that events may bring, librarians need to remain flexible and creative.

REFERENCES

Bromley, Max L. 1984. "Planning for Effective Security at Campus Special Events." *Association of College Unions – International, Bulletin* 52, no. 5 (October): 4–5.

Frank, Donald G., Laura L. Greene, Lisa A. Macklin, Jillian Baker, Tanya Barber, Laurie MacLeod Bennett, Katharine Calhoun, Tom Fisher, and Claire Oslund. 1997. "Life in the Olympic Village: A View from Georgia Tech." *College & Research Libraries News* (May): 319–322.

7 LIBRARY SECURITY: LEGAL, PERSONNEL, AND VENDOR CONSIDERATIONS

LEGAL ISSUES RELATED TO LIBRARY SECURITY

"Society has become very litigious, and because libraries are no longer simply repositories, . . . they are becoming prey to lawsuits. . . . Security concerns breed liability issues." (Switzer, 1999: 165) Some of the legal issues related to security in libraries include:

- Mutilation of material
- Failure to return library materials
- Selling and purchasing materials with ownership markings
- Property liability
- Safe atmosphere for patrons and staff
- Use of surveillance equipment
- Employer responsibility for criminal acts of employees
- Detaining people from exiting
- Negligence about dangerous patrons or staff
- Librarian information malpractice
- Workplace violence
- Employee screening
- Risk management programs
- Insurance
- Sexual harassment
- Copyright (Switzer, 1999: 164–175)

Whether talking about security of the collections, of staff and users, or of data, there are several ways to consider relevant legal issues. These approaches include the institutional context of the library, applicable legal regulations, an overall "plan" for what to do when the system is invoked, and documentation. Having a security plan is not necessary if no action is to be taken when the appropriate conditions invoke it.

INSTITUTIONAL CONTEXT

Libraries vary by type, mission, clientele served, and their relationship with their own governing body. For example, public school libraries ultimately will be responsible to the local city or county school board, preparatory school libraries to their own board of trustees, academic libraries to appropriate vice presidents, and so forth. No matter what the reporting chain, the institutional context of the library should be the driving force behind any procedure involving development and implementation of any security policy or procedures.

Whether the library is developing an overall plan or focusing on specific components, it is a good idea to have a recommended proposal well in mind and committed to paper. This proposal should be clearly delineated with goals stating exactly what the library wants to achieve in specific situations. A typical proposal outline should be followed. That is, terms should be defined, violation examples cited, and suggested outcomes presented. This document should be introduced as a draft of what the library proposes. The draft should conclude with a request for a broad-based security implementation team.

A high-ranking library official should be engaged to provide entree to the identified appropriate legal and local enforcement personnel. Taking this approach allows the legal and local enforcement units to assign the proper people to the security plan implementation team. It also lets other units know the library's preferences early in the process, so time is not wasted trying to communicate unclear goals. By working from such a proposed plan, administrators and legal experts will have an outline of the library's preferences. They will know exactly what the library is trying to achieve. Thus, they will be better able to advise on the appropriateness of the suggested procedures.

For its part, the security planning team should be aware that the document is only a draft. The library must be amenable to all suggestions from the implementation experts. If the expert legal or local enforcement opinion varies too much from the library's goals, that should be a point of discussion rather than a discouragement. The ultimate goal is to have a plan that can be supported at the highest administrative, legal, and local enforcement levels. While identifying the appropriate relevant statutes that cover all aspects of their recommended security plan is possible for librarians, having the assurance that the library's governing arm will support the library is critical. This support can usually be assured by institutional approval.

By way of example of how the institutional context should work with the implementation team, one college library wanted to prosecute anyone caught stealing library materials. However, the college administration, like that of many academic institutions, was not willing or able to arrest students. Administrators wanted to prosecute only community users and to handle students through the student judicial process. In this community, like many, the courts were not willing to prosecute any cases unless they prosecuted all of them. This fact forced the library and the college to analyze their goals in an institutional context and to make a difficult decision. Finally, the decision was made to prosecute all persons under the same circumstances. For this library and others, the decision to proceed was dependent on an institutional context broader than that of the library.

STATE, FEDERAL, AND OTHER APPLICABLE REGULATIONS

Even if the library intends to handle all security violations internally, state and federal laws and ordinances must be satisfied. Robison, Marshall, and Cravey (1992) suggest the following legal areas as being relevant to the development of specific library security plans:

- Distinction between public and private institutions vis-à-vis the Fourteenth Amendment
- "Search" activities sanctioned under the Fourth Amendment
- "Probable cause" as a prerequisite for searches
- Supreme Court exceptions for searches conducted without a warrant
- "Exigent circumstances" regarding evidence that might be lost unless a search without a warrant occurs
- Results of an "illegal search" and possible action for violation of a patron's constitutional rights
- Common-law and statutorily developed torts regarding "false imprisonment" or detainment against a person's will, including the length of time a person may be so detained and the nature of the detention

In addition, several analogous court cases may be applicable in developing a sound legal basis for an overall security program. For example, the use of drug-sniffing dogs, the use of a security alarm system at the exit of a store to prevent shoplifting, and the use of X-ray machines in airports may provide legal interpretations relative to library security. (Robison, Marshall, and Cravey, 1992: 165)

Peripheral issues should be considered as well. For example, in one state, the association regulating contracted security guards let the credentialing standards for such guards elapse. Because of that, anyone was eligible for a security guard position. Until that overlooked piece of legislation was reenacted in the following legislative session, one library in that state was advised not to hire contracted security guards. Regulations might also include the carrying or use of arms, appropriate attire, scope of authority of various types of personnel, and use of police frequency radios. Labor regulations might deal with meals and other breaks, security of the security patrol, the role of the security guard in relation to other nonsecurity duties, and the like. Also, legal issues related to the right of access, surveillance, and patron privacy may vary by jurisdiction. The notions of "sovereign immunity" and "charitable immunity" should also be considered. (Bintliff and Coco, 1984: 103) The web of interdependencies of these regulations, laws, ordinances, rules, and lore makes it difficult for the librarian to stay on top of everything. Librarians should not have to do that. That is why lawyers represent most governing boards.

A library's security program must be developed in compliance with relevant state and federal laws and their interpretations. The use of legal counsel will assure that the proposed policies and procedures are stated in enforceable ways that do not jeopardize the parent organization or the individual staff member. Such protection is enhanced when legal and local enforcement representatives are integral to the planning and implementation teams. Therefore, bringing legal and local enforcement people onto the implementation team in the early planning stage of security program development is essential.

WHAT TO DO WHEN THE PLAN IS INVOKED

Whatever piece of the security picture the library has addressed, and whatever procedures are in place for treating violations, there will come a time when that system will work. That is, someone will violate a library security policy and library staff will apply the procedures. Designing and implementing a system is not the end of the process. Rather, proceeding when the system works is the real challenge.

Written Policies and Procedures

For many reasons, written policies and procedures are essential elements in a conscious overall library security program. These written documents serve the library and its users by assuring all parts of the security program are understood and are carried out consistently. By treating each situation with similar circumstances identically, all people are treated the same without regard for external factors such as race, gender, social class, aroma, attire, fluency in language, and other personal attributes. This sameness is extremely important in a humane environment where people are treated respectfully. For staff charged with implementing procedures, getting caught up in the moment is very easy. It is also easy to forget that the visitor, who has just apparently tried to flash an employee working in the stack area, also has a life and is a real person. Written policies empower staff members to brush aside the normal anxieties a potentially confrontational situation brings and to focus on the facts of that situation.

In addition, written policies and procedures that call for treating like cases in the same manner are critical in a legal context. The Four-

---

Figure 7.1: Sample General Security Statement

To preserve the general collection of the Moran Library, the Circulation Department is charged with responsibility for the security of the general collection. To this end, staff members in that department will follow the procedures outlined in PROCEDURES FOR COLLECTION SECURITY IN THE GENERAL COLLECTION, available in the Library Procedures Manual.
[Date of approval and approval chain information]

---

teenth Amendment contains clauses relating to due process and to equal protection. Further, some library users may be considered to have a contractual relationship with the library or the parent institution. Exclusions or specific legal actions may also create a "breach of contract" situation for these users. Finally, particularly in school or academic libraries, some users may be considered a "protected class." For these people, specific other rights may apply. (Robison, Marshall, and Cravey, 1992: 167–168) These rights also may vary by state interpretation.

Written policies should be tied to the goals and mission of the institution. They should also reflect the laws of the state in which the library is located. The actual policy that is developed can be brief. It should include the approval trail and dates of approval. For example, a policy regarding security of the general collection could be worded as shown in Figure 7.1.

It must also be decided for which pieces of security the various library departments are to be responsible. If one department has overall responsibility for all facets of library security, the policy statement should be clear on that, as shown Figure 7.2. If responsibility for security is distributed among the departments, that fact should be detailed as well. In terms of policies, security should be treated as a broad-based component of the library's overall public services package.

Unlike policies, written procedures provide step-by-step directions for how to handle difficult situations. Procedures should be well writ-

---

Figure 7.2: Sample Specific Policy Statement

Security of library users, staff, and collections in the Butler Library is the responsibility of the Public Services Division. Thus, appropriate staff in that division will follow the procedures outlined in PROCEDURES FOR LIBRARY SECURITY, available in the Office of the Head Librarian.
[Date of approval and approval chain information]

---

ten and clear. Staff should test the procedures and suggest changes in them until the procedures are workable for the specific circumstances at each institution. For example, written procedures for collection security managed by an electronic book-theft-detection system could include the following components:

- What to do and say when the alarm sounds
- What to check
- Where to search
- Whom to call
- How long the search can go on (determined by police procedures, if police are involved)
- What reports need to be completed and by whom
- Where the reports go
- Who is responsible for assuring the reports are properly processed
- What will happen if there is or is not an arrest
- Going to court
- Following up on court cases
- What to do for items that are being removed intact from the library
- Definition of mutilation
- Who will determine when something is mutilated
- Procedures for items that are mutilated
- Procedures to be followed for all user statuses

The actual procedure manual for any piece of the security package will be quite lengthy and repetitive. However, it should not include cross-references. Repeat the step-by-step directions rather than saying, for example, "Refer to page 20, item 4, and repeat this procedure." Remembering that the person on the front line is feeling enormous pressure is important, so the procedures must be very clear. It is also useful to place a "cheat sheet" or flow chart summary at the front of each manual so experienced staff members can use it for quick referral. Again, administrators and legal people who know exactly what the library is trying to achieve will be better able to advise on the appropriateness of the suggested procedures.

Security of the collection is only a small part of the total security picture. Written procedures for personal and physical security should be as detailed as they are for collections. (Elder, 1986; George, 1994) Creating a detailed procedure manual for all aspects of the library security program is one of the most difficult and time-consuming parts of developing an in-depth security plan. If done thoroughly and with the advice of legal and administrative sources, such a manual will be the backbone of the security program.

Training for Staff and Users

As with most important initiatives, a well-developed program to explain to staff and library constituents the particulars of the new security program will go a long way to creating the proper atmosphere.

For staff, training and role-playing should be undertaken until all staff members who will be responsible for carrying out the new program are comfortable with its procedures. Depending on the time allotted for this training each day and the complexity of the procedures to be learned, this training could take one to two weeks. Intense training can create much anxiety on the part of the employees. Trainers should be sensitive to this possibility. After the responsible staff members have been trained, presentations should be made to the rest of the library indicating how the new policies and procedures will be implemented. A few "case studies" should be demonstrated. These case studies should show both the typical responses from a user and the appropriate responses from the newly trained staff member. It is important to communicate that this is a serious part of the library's customer service package. The rest of the library must understand the stresses that the trained staff members will bear. Security is not a joke. For example, triggering devices or targets should not be hidden in other employees' belongings as "a joke." Setting someone up in such a way is disrespectful to the colleague as well as the staff member who will then have the stressful task of carrying out the difficult procedure.

Many parent institutions offer classes or training sessions on such serious topics as physical and verbal assault, diversity, and substance abuse. Such classes also help sensitize staff to the emotional and physical needs of people who have been violated in these specific personal or physical ways. It is insufficient to follow step-by-step procedures to protect the library's interests without demonstrating genuine concern for the victim's needs as well. Patrons must feel comfortable reporting incidents in private. They need to know their situations will be addressed in a professional manner, confidentially, and with sensitivity. Staff workshops can go a long way to improving relations within the security context.

Users, too, will need to know that the library is serious about security—that the new procedures have been approved by both the legal and enforcement units of the parent institution. Articles in local papers or institutional newsletters, pamphlets, flyers, Web pages, and the like may be used to publicize the new program. One library found it useful to present the new procedures to the public by tying them to the appropriate state statute. Signs were placed on each floor of the library indicating the legal basis for the new program. Figure 7.3 is an example of such a statement. The legal arm of the institution should review all signs and make appropriate suggestions. Also, signs and

---

Figure 7.3: Sample Generic Legal Statement

According to State Statute Number ST-431, it is illegal to steal library materials. Persons who violate this statute may be arrested.

---

policies tied to statutes should be updated if the statute number or its content change.

One interesting aspect of increasing security is with visibility. As users see action being taken to increase security in the library, their sense of how seriously the library views security is heightened. Observing the proper implementation of the security program is one excellent training tool for users.

Specific Instructions for Each Staff Group

In addition to the security program's policies and comprehensive step-by-step procedures manual, specific instructions should be prepared for each involved staff group. These instructions should become an integral part of the manual. For example, one part of this section of the manual should include what the chief library administrator is expected to do in specific situations. Another section should include step-by-step directions for front-line staff. A third section should cite what the library can expect from the enforcement unit. By including these directions for specific staff groups, as well as the overall procedures manual and the "cheat sheet," staff can review the relevant parts of the program whenever time permits. Breaking out the procedures in this way also makes the overall process seem much less formidable.

Provide Specific Proof of Ownership

Each item belonging to the library should be marked with permanent ownership markings. Bookplates, call numbers, and bar code labels can be removed with varying degrees of ease. Some libraries write the call number inside the book in a specific location, some have an accession number stamped in a uniform place, others have a special stamp at a regular spot in each book. These innocuous markings give additional ownership credibility to the library. Their absence may also highlight "probable cause" and "intent to steal" situations. One very effective method of identifying ownership has been to stamp the three edges of each book with an ink stamp. The more of each book's edges consumed by the stamp, the easier it is to prove ownership. This could be a good place to use a stamp with the library's full name and institution or city. Slow times at service desks are an opportune time to stamp the edges of new books or books being discharged. The stamped edges have the added advantage of easy visual recognition during a routine check of someone's book bag. These additional processing steps are worth the investment in staff time.

One library also uses a one-inch-wide stripe along one edge of each unbound periodical issue. This stripe is hardly noticed by the user and has had enormous advantages in identifying the single periodical article taken from an issue. By matching the stripe on the article with the stripe on the unbound issue, the library will most surely have probable cause to prove the user is carrying library property. The colored stripe also makes it easier to prove an entire unbound issue belongs to the library even if the mailing label has been removed and the patron insists it is a personal copy recently purchased at a bookstore. Again, the stripe enhances visual inspection of the contents of a briefcase. The user may have honestly picked up a periodical issue and included it with a jumble of papers. One issue can be quickly spotted. As long as the issue is not mutilated, the user can be allowed to proceed through the exit.

Media items and other ephemera are more difficult to protect in this way. However, many of them can be targeted with commercially prepared devices to activate an electronic theft-detection system. In some cases, however, electromagnetic systems may damage media materials. (Mason-Robinson, 1996: 78) Other types of ownership markings on media are difficult to design. One interesting fact about library videos, however, is that commercial video rental stores usually have price bar codes that contain the security device. Library users frequently assume the library media bar codes work the same way. If libraries can design security systems that have the alarm trigger separate from the bar code, security of media items will be enhanced.

Concealment as Evidence of Intent to Steal

If the library is concerned about theft of library materials, then the security definitions should include mention of concealment. Concealment may be related to theft of materials by way of mutilation. Conversely, in some legal instances, mutilation may be considered a form of concealment. Thus, library security definitions should also include a definition of mutilation. Many jurisdictions consider mutilation to be an "active crime." That is, mutilation can only be charged or proven when the act of mutilating was actually observed. To accommodate this legal requirement, the library's security manual may have to describe "evidence of mutilation" as an indicator of intent to steal. Because of this, examples of what may constitute mutilation should also be included in the manual. In terms of legal issues related to library security, there are two types of concealment.

The first type of concealment occurs when library property is found among the user's property or in clothing or accessories. One example of this type of concealment is a periodical article found in a wallet. In this case, the user probably removed the article and folded it to fit into the wallet. The library was lucky because the trigger device for the electronic security system was attached to one page of the article. Another example of this type of concealment may be a periodical article tucked among the disarray of papers in a briefcase. In this situation, the user may hope that the employee thinks the messy pile is such a jumble that there could be nothing there. It would be nice for the patron if the employee did not check things out too thoroughly. Alternatively, the user could say the article was "picked up by mistake" when personal belongings were scooped into a backpack in the rush to get to the next appointment.

The second type of concealment is related to mutilation. It occurs when the user removes and tries to hide some of the parts that identify the item as belonging to the library. For example, patrons often think the trigger device is in the bar code of the book. Consequently, they remove the bar code from the book. If the removed bar code can be found within the building quickly, that is excellent evidence of intent to steal. In one library there is a "15 minute" rule. That is how long searching for evidence can continue before the patron needs to be charged or released. While this rigid local police department rule may seem to constrain staff in their ability to find evidence, a team of skilled searchers nevertheless embarks on a search for each situation. One of the first places they look is in areas near where the book would normally have been shelved. Frequently the evidence is found on a high empty shelf, or on top of or stuck under a nearby study table or chair. In one case, the person who was assigned to search for the missing bar code went up one flight of stairs before she realized she did not have the book's call number with her. She turned to return to the circulation desk to obtain the call number. As she did so, she discovered the book's bar code label on top of a light fixture in the stairwell about eight feet from the exit! The label could only be seen as a person was descending the first few steps. Seeing the label during an ascent was impossible. This evidence provided all that was necessary to obtain a positive probable cause hearing result. Another library provides gloves so trash containers that are located near the book's proper home can be searched. Thorough searching for evidence might also include study areas near where the book would have been shelved, telephone booths, individual study rooms, bathrooms, and under loose tiles. When fully staffed, one large department can search an entire 11–story library building in about 12 minutes. More often than not, the evidence is found.

Call number labels, bookplates, book covers, and date due slips can all be removed in order to steal materials. However, evidence of their

---

Figure 7.4: Sample Specific Legal Statement

Proof of concealment shall be *prima facie* evidence of intent to steal.

---

removal remains in most items. When pieces of evidence are found and match perfectly with the remaining markings on the book, the police take the situation seriously. Also, refusing to prosecute anyone for whom there is no corroborating evidence found reinforces the seriousness with which the institution takes its searches.

If concealment legally is considered as an aspect of theft, the library-wide signs that tie the security program to the state statutes might need to be amended. For example, a sentence could be added, as shown in Figure 7.4.

False Alarms

Fear of confrontation is a serious problem in library security. In many libraries with electronic book-theft-detection systems, for example, fear of confrontation leads to staff shrugging their shoulders and saying, "It must be a false alarm." If that is how alarms are to be handled once an electronic system is installed, there is no point in spending the money on such a system. If a library intends to have a security program, it must plan seriously for what to do when the system works.

There really is no such thing as a "false alarm." Something is causing the electronic system to respond. "False alarm" is the current buzzword used for those times when the system alarms but no one is willing to try to resolve the situation. For example, if a non-library book is the only thing a person is carrying, that book should be checked as a possible cause of the alarm. It may be a book from a nearby bookstore that has a device in it that will cause the library alarm system to sound. This is not a false alarm. If the book definitely does not belong to the library, the trigger should be deactivated. In this way the patron will be spared future embarrassment and delay. If the alleged book sensor is thus disengaged and the alarm sounds again when the patron passes through the exit, this is still not a false alarm. Something else is causing the alarm to sound.

Items to investigate as possible causes of the alarm include:

- Video from commercial video places
- Large wads of keys
- Calculators in the "on" position
- Essays or articles that have been removed from a periodical and

hidden in a wallet or blazer pocket, but which still have an active security target intact
- Other non-library products

Staff members in one library have found hairline-sized devices in new drug store products that are still shrink wrapped, such as on a bottle of eye drops or on a box of tampons. As well, triggering devices have been found in beautiful leather diaries and stuck on the bottoms of shoes. These are also not false alarms. They are real alarms caused by non-library products. Staff should investigate until the cause of the alarm is found. Commercial video cases that trigger the alarm should be investigated to assure they do not contain library videos. It is important to determine the cause of each alarm and then to fix the problem. This thoroughness serves the patron better in the long run.

Another reason to keep investigating until the cause of the alarm is located is to find out if the system is malfunctioning. Occasionally a system has seemed to sound for umbrellas and briefcases. In those cases, a pattern may be determined and reported to the service center. For example, one system had hundreds of alarms on rainy days. It seemed that umbrellas were causing the system to sound. Soon, anyone with an umbrella was waved out the door with an apology and the words, "false alarm, sorry." No one bothered to investigate each alarm to be sure there were no library materials concealed within the umbrellas or in the person's belongings. As it turned out, the system was not calibrated correctly and the humidity on rainy days was causing a system malfunction. It was not the umbrellas at all, but a call for system repair.

There was once a model of briefcase that had a specific, metallic-design feature that actually did cause a system to alarm. Because of its insistence on exploring all alarms, the library could determine which model briefcase caused the alarm. If a patron set off the security system and was carrying such a briefcase, after a thorough search of the case to assure no library materials were being compromised, the entire briefcase was desensitized. This was physically a bit awkward, but resulted in the patron not being inconvenienced after that initial wait. There is no need to hear a patron say: "Oh, the alarm always sounds when I exit." Staff members should figure out why the alarm is sounding and fix the problem. Real solutions represent far better service than a smiling "false alarm" statement. It is important to remember that security is an integral part of the library's service package.

It is also a good idea, once an alarm has sounded, not to allow persons who set off the alarm to leave the area until the cause of the alarm has been determined. Many times as soon as the alarm sounds, patrons turn around and declare they have to go to the bathroom, they left their laptop on an upper floor, or they forgot they were to meet their mother at another place. Usually when this happens, concealed and/or mutilated items are found in the person's possession. In most jurisdictions, it is appropriate to detain the patron long enough to determine the cause of the alarm. The fact that the alarm sounds provides probable cause.

DOCUMENTATION

At some point during the development of a security plan, the documentation will seem to take over! Documentation is a necessary part of "getting it right." Each security situation that meets the library's criteria for a security incident should be documented. For example, documentation should be prepared for all incidents involving theft of personal property or physical abuse. However, if a library uses an electronic book-theft-detection system, documenting each alarm of the gate would be ludicrous. Instead, the procedures for gate alarms should dictate which situations are security breaches. Each type of security breach will probably have its own required documentation.

Relevant documents for each situation should be compiled into a file. Complete files about each case are important, as they provide feedback, serve as a memory jog, and allow for the compilation of statistics on the activity of the overall security program. Since it may take many months to resolve a case, a complete file is essential to recall the details of each case.

Finally, a secure place to store the documents and files is necessary. The legal arm of the parent institution should advise the library on the types of documentation to maintain for each case and on how long these documents should be retained. Having a file for cases that are "closed" probably will be necessary. While records for closed cases may not legally need to be retained for very long after the case is resolved, the library may prefer to keep these records as an archive of the security program. Also, a file for cases that are still "active" is critical. How long an "active" case should remain active, even if there is no legal activity, may vary by jurisdiction. For example, an "active" case that resulted in an arrest may need to remain "active" until it is closed at the court level.

Meanwhile, the library may choose to have someone assigned the task of researching the "active" cases several times per year to see if any are closed. In more and more jurisdictions these files are online. If the local courts are being used for the cases, sometimes cases are resolved without notification to the library. In those instances, a case could sit in the library's "active" file with the related evidence out of circulation much longer than is necessary. An occasional trip to the

---

Figure 7.5: Buffered Narrative Report #1

The suspect remarked that she brought the book into the library and that it belongs to another library.

---

court to check on these cases frequently gives closure to a burgeoning file of unresolved papers or to an unwieldy stack of evidence. In academic settings, a check with the honor courts or dean's office could also close cases for which the library has not been previously notified.

Evidence should be stored until a case is resolved. Repairing an item damaged in a security case prior to the conclusion of the case may invalidate the evidence. While the policy to retain evidence until then may frustrate patrons and librarians alike, retaining it is essential to the successful case outcome. However, evidence should be released as soon as the case is closed. Reports, forms, and checklists are components of incident documentation.

Reports

Reports should include as much information as possible about each incident. Every staff member involved must prepare an individually written report of what is known firsthand. Involved staff members should not be allowed to compare versions of the incident prior to writing their reports. "Law enforcement does not want a consensus of what happened. It is important that observations of each individual be assessed independently." (Clark, 1998: 40) Reports from individual staff members should include only facts. Necessary inclusions usually are date, time, place, and a description of what was done and how it tied into the written procedures. Comments on what the user said can also be included. Such comments, however, are best stated in a buffered way. For example, the report could include a statement similar to that in Figure 7.5 or Figure 7.6.

Buffering the verbiage takes the library employee away from presenting the suspect's words as direct quotes. Testifying to direct quotes that may be inaccurate could lead to lost opportunities.

Reports should not include impressions (for example, "The suspect acted as if he were on drugs."). This kind of evaluative statement could call into question the staff member's medical credentials. Nor should

---

Figure 7.6: Buffered Narrative Report #2

The suspect said something like: "I found it on the shelf without the cover."

Figure 7.7: Sample Inappropriate Report Text

The suspect in this case was sitting on the floor and using a mirror to look up ladies' skirts. He was wearing the same clothes as last week when he was also apprehended for exposing himself in the government documents area.

---

reports include known facts unrelated to the case. Figure 7.7 is an example of an inappropriate statement.

Staff members may be assigned to search the library for evidence of a security breach. For example, in one library, if the cover is missing from a book that sets off the security system alarm, the assumption is that the user removed the cover to steal the book. However, that library will not press charges unless some evidence of the crime is found. To that end, all available staff members fan out into the library searching for the missing cover. If it is found, it is called evidence, and the security policy is invoked.

Employees who search and staff who find the cover each prepare a report. The unsuccessful searcher's report could be brief; Figure 7.8 is an example. The successful searcher's report, on the other hand, should provide much more detail. An example appears in Figure 7.9. All the reports from everyone involved in each case should be merged into an information packet that is made available to the responsible parties. This information packet becomes the core of the official documentation. The legal and enforcement arms will dictate exactly what is to be included in an information packet, and where it should go when completed.

Deadlines for when the information packets have to be received by the next administrative level should be spelled out. While 24 hours may seem to be a reasonable time frame for completion of information packets, that may be unrealistic if the library is open weekend or evening hours. For example, when the process is being managed by an employee who is protected under the Wage and Hour Law, expecting that employee to complete a report within 24 hours could be unrealistic. If the event occurs on the last day of the pay period and at closing, completing a report within the pay week will be impossible.

Figure 7.8: Unsuccessful Searcher's Report

I was asked by [name of responsible staff member] to search for evidence in the security case at 9:15 P.M. on [DATE]. I searched the 7th floor in the stacks areas where the book would normally have been shelved and did not find the cover.

Figure 7.9: Successful Searcher's Report
[Name of staff member] asked me to search for evidence in the security case on [DATE] at 9:15 P.M. I went to the children's department reading well on the first floor and found the cover to the book in a trash can on the west wall near the bathrooms. I gave the evidence to [name of staff member].

In absence of an overtime policy for such cases, a reasonable time frame must be allowed. One library includes a copy of the police report in each information packet. The amount of time necessary to obtain such a report may also dictate how quickly the information packets can be available.

There may be different laws governing reports about incidents involving juveniles. It is important that the legal advisors are aware that juveniles might be involved.

Forms

Forms are often useful for standardizing processes. By using forms, staff members are able to focus on the content of their reports rather than on worrying about an appropriate format. An array of forms may be useful to complete the reporting process. Thus, a series of templates may be designed as forms for the various reports. Templates may be necessary for reports written by each person who searched for evidence, by the person who found the evidence, by the staff member responsible for coordinating the incident response team, and by the person to whom the incident was reported. If additional staff witnessed an incident, those witness reports should also be included on individual forms. All these reports and their related forms are designed to be internal documents; they are not meant to replace official police reports. Furthermore, they are not designed to accompany police reports and probably should not be offered to the police.

A permission form may be necessary to authorize someone to go to the police office and obtain a copy of the official police report. This form may need to be designed by a representative of the police jurisdiction. A public library will work out a plan with their local police precinct. In an academic library, the form can be designed with the campus police. Even with a permission form, the person retrieving the police report may need to present personal identification. In an academic or school setting, there may be specific forms necessary to refer student offenders to the dean or to the student judicial system.

Many libraries have a policy of excusing one nonviolent offense before taking official action. In these cases, the library must design a form to record a first offense. A note in an electronic patron record would meet that requirement. If this system is used, staff must remember to check the file each time before deciding what action is appropriate. This means the file must be available at all hours the library is open.

Forms should also be designed to record the results of court appearances and the outcome of each case. In one library, a form is also used to inform the technical services department about periodicals that are being held as evidence. This form then triggers staff to enter information into the online record that the issue is unavailable as it is being held as evidence. Once the case is settled, the same form can accompany the evidence back to the periodicals department to help them in adjusting the record and to alert them to any repairs that might be needed.

Finally, a cover letter form is useful for the entire information packet. A complete copy of the information packet should be retained in the department charged with managing the security program. In addition, copies should be sent wherever procedures dictate. Several cover letter forms may be needed, depending on the outcome of each case. In most cases, the cover letter should be short; the enclosed reports should provide all the information necessary. In one library, the original information packet is retained in the department charged in the library policy statement with managing the security program, a copy of the entire information packet with a cover letter is sent to the library's administrative office, and a second copy is sent to the institution's internal legal office. An example of a cover letter that follows these procedures appears in Figure 7.10.

Checklists

A variety of checklists may also be developed to expedite completion of the requisite documentation for each case. When properly designed, a checklist may serve many purposes. For example, two important uses of checklists may be for processing steps and for case outcomes.

A checklist of all required processing steps is useful because it can serve as a quick summary of all the steps necessary to complete a case record. A processing checklist also assures that all such steps have been completed. If copies of the information packets are to be routed to others, a processing steps checklist can either accompany the cover letter for the routed packets or it can be an integral part of the cover letter. Either way, administrators and local legal representatives will be assured that all the appropriate steps for processing a case have been completed. The checklist should reflect the procedures outlined in the library's overall security plan. A processing checklist that is not an integral part of the cover letter might look like the example in Figure 7.11.

Figure 7.10: Sample Cover Letter

TO: [Name of next level library official]

FROM: [Name of the person designated to be in charge of security cases in the library policy statement]

SUBJECT: Security case involving [Name of patron]

DATE: [Date information packet is to be sent]

    Enclosed please find the information packet compiled for the security case occurring on [DATE] and involving [Patron Name]. This person [name the result here, for example: was arrested.]

CC: [Copies may need to be sent to the legal arm of the parent institution.]

Checklists can also be developed to include a list of outcomes. In a formal reporting system, these closed cases should be filed separately from the current, or "active," cases. In a paper-based system, the checklist of outcomes can be printed on a different color paper and be placed on top of the information packet and file for each closed case.

Situations that might cause a case to be closed include:

- Inability to prosecute, including a lack of evidence
- Special ruling, such as a first-offender program that is successfully completed
- A legal ruling such as a "guilty" or "not guilty" pronouncement from a judge
- An unsuccessful probable cause hearing

Some libraries, for statistical purposes, also keep track of situations where the offender is "anonymous" and no further action can be taken. For juveniles, the court system has different standards. Typically a juvenile offender will be asked to do something specific, like write an essay, for the judge. The library will have little involvement in a juvenile case and it will quickly be closed.

A checklist of outcomes will allow statistical data to be collected on each case in order to facilitate reporting security procedure results. The contents of a checklist of outcomes should be relevant for each library. Such a checklist might resemble the example in Figure 7.12.

Figure 7.11: Sample Processing Steps Checklist

NAME OF LIBRARY
NAME OF DEPARTMENT
TITLE OF DOCUMENT [Processing Steps Checklist]

Name of user involved in incident: _____

Date of incident: _____

Name of responsible staff member: _____

List of steps to be followed:
_____ Report from responsible staff member
_____ Reports from additional employees [#]
_____ Bill sent
_____ Police report
_____ Note added to patron record
_____ Technical services notified
_____ Reference notified
_____ Item charged to "evidence"
_____ Whatever else the institution wants in a report, listed as separate items

---

Figure 7.12: Sample Outcomes Checklist

NAME OF LIBRARY
NAME OF DEPARTMENT
TITLE OF REPORT [Outcomes Checklist]

The following case was closed on [DATE], because: _____

_____.

Name of person involved: _____

Date of the case: _____

_____ Evidence discharged/sent to appropriate place
_____ Reports moved to closed file
_____ Patron record noted that the case is now closed

PERSONNEL ISSUES RELATED TO LIBRARY SECURITY

Four issues relating to employees and security impact personnel practices and the law. First, laws, amendments, and legal interpretations that define appropriate employment processes are continuously changing and being refined. Second, incidents of employee theft and other employee crimes continue to rise in all businesses. Libraries are no exception. "Inside jobs are no doubt the most difficult acts to interdict or prevent because employees are normally spared the careful scrutiny accorded members of the public in their visits to the building." (Shuman, 1999: 192) Third, employers are often held liable for the actions of their employees. Finally, matters of employee safety and workplace violence are receiving often-sensationalized press coverage. These matters should be taken seriously despite the sensationalized coverage. (Switzer, 1999: 37–49) Laws increasingly encroach on all aspects of workplace management. It is no longer possible to select personnel based on an administrative "gut" feeling that this applicant "seems" fine. Neither is it acceptable to select an applicant based on family friendships. For these reasons, and others, legal issues related to personnel and library security must be considered at the design phase of the library's employment practices, policies, and procedures.

Major laws affecting employment practices comprise the most critical issues related to a wide variety of personnel matters. These laws can be divided into four groups. (Purpura, 1989: 132–133) The first group consists of antidiscrimination laws. These laws encompass the Civil Rights Act of 1964 and its amendments, including the Equal Employment Opportunity Act. Other antidiscrimination laws are the Americans with Disabilities Act and the Age Discrimination in Employment Act. The second group of laws regulating hiring practices includes those governing issues related to wages, benefits, and working conditions. Most notable in this category are the Federal Insurance Contributions Act and the Occupational Safety and Health Act and its amendments and interpretations. A third group of important laws impacting personnel matters relates to privacy. The Fair Credit Reporting Act and the Privacy Act are included in this group. State laws affecting the use of polygraph results are also included in this category. The final group of laws impacting employment issues can be termed miscellaneous. Among these are the National Labor Relations Act, state and federal guidelines for the use of information regarding prior criminal activities and convictions, guidelines for the use of signed waiver forms, and the Drug Free Workplace Act. (Bielefield and Cheeseman, 1993;

Layne, 1994a: 3) Interpretation of the correct use of these laws, amendments, acts, and guidelines may vary by state.

In most libraries, the application of many of these policies is dictated by the parent institution. Procedures, however, may be allowed to vary. Relevant aspects of personnel issues and their relationships to the overall security program include hiring, employee policies, and termination procedures.

HIRING

In addition to being used to select the best person for each vacant position, sound hiring practices may be viewed as a "major loss prevention tactic." (Purpura, 1989: 129) Administrators should look at employees both as people to carry out the security policy and as security risks. Careful adherence to legal issues related to hiring can protect the organization.

The first step is to design a standard application form. An attorney should screen the form to make sure that the questions asked violate no laws. All applicants, even those who submit a resume, should complete a standard application form. Application forms have the advantage of standardizing the information requested from each applicant. If all applicants submit standardized application forms, information on resumes can be considered separately from the application information. In some organizations, permanent employees are required to undergo rigorous investigation, but temporary employees and volunteers are not. Ideally, all libraries should have specific hiring guidelines for all employees, regardless of employment status. (Layne, 1994a: 1)

Preemployment screening can lead to better-qualified employees who are not risks for the organization. Experts increasingly endorse comprehensive preemployment screening. Most responsible hiring officials now screen potential employees in a variety of ways, including:

- Personal interview
- Telephone interview
- Predictive testing
- Polygraph testing
- Psychological stress evaluators
- Contacts with a variety of work-related and personal references
- Handwriting analysis
- Investigation of driving records
- Exploration of worker compensation records

Increasingly, states require criminal background checks for job applicants before a final offer is extended for employment into state agencies. Many institutions also require drug testing. In cases where personnel handle money, credit checks are required. Some crime prevention experts suggest a full background check that includes surveying the applicant's neighborhood for inconsistencies. For example, an expensive car that does not match the neighborhood or an expensive home that does not match the job for which the applicant is interviewing could be red flags for hiring officials. (Layne, 1994b: 2) The thorough screening of applicants can add substantial time to the hiring process and may result in the loss of potentially excellent employees to organizations that do not screen as thoroughly. However, such screening protects the organization from both direct loss and litigation losses relative to carelessness in the hiring procedures. Whatever methods are chosen for selecting and screening applicants, they must be applied uniformly and must meet the legal requirements of the parent organization and the jurisdiction of the library.

All applicants should have a clear understanding of what will be expected of them regarding the library's security program. These expectations should be listed in the job advertisement and discussed in the personal interview. Candidates for positions should have copies of the written expectations for the position. They should also have a report of the employer's responsibility for security. While this approach may sound severe and may actually discourage some applicants, it does provide protection to the library by screening out possible staff members who are uncomfortable with such a level of scrutiny. Once a new employee is selected and "signed," other policies and procedures related to employment apply.

EMPLOYMENT POLICIES AND PROCEDURES

To protect the institution and its employees, policies and procedures about all phases of employment are generally dictated by the parent organization; all such policies and procedures should also be reviewed by the appropriate legal sources before enactment. The final approved version of these policies and procedures should be in writing. Copies should be presented to all new employees no later than their first day of employment. "People are basically honest and will remain that way if they know they are working for a concerned and well-run organization." (Seedman, 1989: 431) Among the legal issues to consider in an employment plan are standards, expectations, evaluations, and disciplinary procedures.

Standards

Both employee conduct within the organization and organizational obligations to the employee should be addressed in written standards. Such organizational standards with regard to security must be very specific. Legal approval for these written standards should also be sought. Shuman (1999: 192) suggests some standards libraries should consider in developing employee programs designed to complement the plan to prevent, detect, and punish employee misconduct. These standards include:

- A written code of acceptable employee behavior
- Awareness by staff that criminal activity within the workplace will lead to dismissal and may lead to arrest
- A consistent plan to prosecute evidence of employee malfeasance
- A plan to limit access to supplies
- A plan to block long-distance calling

The library also has obligations to its employees with regard to security. The library is required to maintain a safe work environment and to do everything possible to see that the environment remains safe during the employment period. Certainly, selecting appropriate staff is one way libraries protect their employees. Training is another way. Training on security issues should be required for all employees. Training should encompass both personal safety and security as well as employee responsibilities related to the overall security program for the library. Additionally, attending refresher classes sponsored by the employer should be a regular part of the employee's responsibilities. Training should "review stress indicators, documentation requirements, and reporting procedures." (Layne, 1994b: 1) Laws support thorough initial training programs and training refresher programs. Lack of a comprehensive training plan and periodic refreshers could lead to viable claims of negligent training. (Studies, 1995) Thus, training also protects the organization.

Expectations

New staff should arrive with a clear understanding of what will be expected of them regarding the library's overall security program. When new employees begin work, they should be given written statements of behavioral policies and procedures, including those related to the overall security program. These statements should be read to the new staff member and discussed point by point in the presence of a witness. New employees and all witnesses should then sign the document. The signed document should become a part of the employee's permanent personnel file. The employee should also be given a personal copy to retain. Further, if it is not a part of the behavioral policy, new employees should be given a statement on disciplinary procedures that the library will employ. These disciplinary procedures will assure the employee and the institution that certain behaviors will be treated in certain ways. Acts that would result in a patron's arrest, for example, should be treated the same way for staff members. (Lincoln, 1984: 146) Such a document also should list the employees' rights to due process. (Layne, 1994a: 19)

On the flip side, the library should provide all employees with lockers or other lockable safe places to store personal belongings. The rules for storing items in these secure places should also be included.

In addition to physical safety, good faith efforts to see that the employee succeeds will go a long way toward reducing the possibility of employee crime. Removing such barriers to success as good-old-boy networks, glass ceilings, the rigid corporate culture, the long-standing structure of communications, fear of downsizing, negative stereotypes, and the lack of advancement opportunities could reap significant rewards for the library. (Bassman, 1992: 28–38) Mentoring programs and other proactive programs that foster success and employee buy-in, have all been successful in several major U.S. corporations.

Evaluations

Formal, regular, written job performance evaluations are an essential procedure. The parent institution's legal counsel should review the standard evaluation forms. The supervisor's written evaluation, on the approved forms, should be reviewed by the appropriate administrative personnel before being read by the employee. This administrative review assures balance in the document. Successes and infractions should be documented in the evaluation. Suggestions for improvement should also be provided. Evaluations should be viewed as an avenue to resolve bidirectional issues. Besides representing sound legal methodology for employee dismissal, performance evaluations can also temper poor performance and point the way to acceptable performance. As a part of the overall security plan, employees also should be evaluated on their contributions to the security program. This assessment should include mention of the employee's adherence to the written guidelines for employee performance as well as behavior in the public program, if that is a part of the job.

Disciplinary Procedures

Disciplinary procedures for people caught stealing materials are explained as a part of the public security program. Further, disciplinary procedures should be spelled out for employees involved in the security program and in the overall security plan for the library. Some possible disciplinary outcomes for criminal activity by employees could include:

- Stern warning

- Referral to psychological counseling
- Probation
- Suspension
- Transfer within the organization
- Demotion with reduction in salary
- Publicity within the organization
- Termination
- Criminal prosecution (Shuman, 1999: 193)

Again, procedures for enacting most of these disciplinary possibilities should be worked out with an attorney representing the parent institution. Employees should be very clear in their understanding of the possibilities. A wealth of risk management literature (for example, Harold, 1989: 179–186) provides many examples of questions to consider in designing internal theft-reduction programs.

TERMINATION

Sometimes, no matter how hard the organization tries to salvage a relationship, the employee is unable to meet the standards and expectations of the organization, or the organization is unable to meet the employee's expectations. In these cases, termination of the relationship may be necessary. A humane termination policy can "lessen negative feelings among those fired." (Shuman, 1999: 195) The goal of termination should be to end the relationship efficiently and to point the employee in a different direction. Procedures for ending employment should also be written, accessible to the employee, and reviewed by legal counsel. Lawyers representing the library should be involved, behind the scenes if possible, in any termination process. Processes in the procedure manual must be followed to the letter. In all cases of employee termination, but especially in cases of disgruntled employees, several areas must be considered critical to the safety and security of the remaining employees. Keys, access codes, electronic passwords, and the right to return to the library must be considered and dealt with at the point of termination.

Keys and Access Codes

Retrieving all keys issued to terminating employees is essential to the safety of the remaining employees and for the security of library materials. The penalty for lost keys should be stiff enough that staff members are encouraged not to "lose" keys. Administrators should consider changing locks if keys are lost. In fact, it is a good idea to change locks every two years whether or not keys have been lost. In institutions where the budget does not allow this expense, locks can be swapped.

If employees have card access to the building or any special areas, the departing staff member's access number should be erased immediately. Also, combinations on safes should be changed if the departing staff member had access to any such combinations.

Electronic Passwords

In one library-related organization, if an employee is about to be fired, the removal of all electronic passwords and the final conference coincide. Thus, when terminated employees return from the termination conference, they can no longer log into the system. This keeps disgruntled employees from making e-mail threats to other employees or from compromising systems. Electronic passwords should be deactivated immediately.

Returning to the Library

Some employees should not, under any circumstances, be permitted to return to the former place of employment. Such injunction is especially necessary for a disgruntled staff member whose employment has been terminated. As a condition of termination, employees should be told in writing if they cannot return to the library. For many library situations, this prohibition will probably need to specify an expiration date. To avoid charges of favoritism or discrimination, the library's personnel manual should list specific occasions when a terminated employee might have to be prohibited from returning to the library. In a school or academic library, a prohibition of this nature may need to be arranged with the attorney if the person in question is also a student. In public libraries, other legal arrangements may be necessary for branches within a system.

There is a broad range of opinion on how personnel matters affect library security. Also, many different issues must be considered with legal representatives before establishing appropriate programs for employee recruitment, placement, success, and termination. Safety and security of the library's employees include hiring matters, appropriate supervision during the employment period, and sound termination practices. Issues of workplace violence and employee theft consume many lines of print in management literature as well. These issues can be dealt with by employing legally sound and humane employment practices.

SECURITY CONSULTANT AND VENDOR SELECTION ISSUES

There are many legal aspects to hiring security consultants and commercial vendors, all very specific to the required protocol at individual libraries or to their parent institutions. In addition, federal, state, and local laws govern procedures for contracting consultants and vendors, particularly for publicly supported institutions. In some cases, relevant legislation may even vary from one legislative session to another within the same state. Amendments and legal interpretations also impact the process. Further, credentialing regulations will influence the engagement of such outside assistance. Insurance issues must be resolved. Bid writing will also be a part of the placement procedures. Finally, licensing agreements are necessary to protect both the interests of the vendor and those of the institution. For these reasons and others, employing security consultants and engaging commercial vendors should be coordinated with the legal arm of the parent organization.

Library security is different from other types of security assignments. For example, buildings are open, browsing is encouraged, floors are frequently not staffed, and there are many nooks and crannies where undesirable behavior may take place. Consequently, outside contractors employed for library security purposes should be experienced in library security matters. Libraries should select security consultants from an array of possibilities. Layne (1994a: 14), an experienced library security consultant, suggests several items that should be included in considerations for hiring all such consultants. The following elements comprise his list:

- Detailed specifications for what the library expects from the security consultant
- A list of professional qualities the bidders will need to bring to the assignment
- A pre-bid conference
- A fair adjustment period
- Open and clear communications
- Thorough reference checking
- Personnel conferences
- Review of objectives and procedures
- Evaluation of action plans, such as those for system functioning, guard orders, and the like
- Personnel selection
- Inspection
- Review

Considering these elements should result in a "viable contract to reach the necessary objectives of solid security, reduced liability, and protection of adjacent properties." (Layne, 1997: 47)

SECURITY CONSULTANT

Library security consultants may be used for:

- Conducting a security audit
- Developing an overall security plan
- Planning a piece of the program's implementation
- Evaluating the success of a trial plan
- Completing a cost analysis
- Any of a variety of other evaluative duties

Many types of people can be contracted to serve as security consultants. These types range from librarians who have had considerable experience in security matters, to local police officers, to certified protection professionals. The library's budget and goals for the consultant will determine which type of employee will do the best job for the situation. The most important requirement for a security consultant is a written, detailed list of the library's expectations for the consultant. Certainly what the library wants the security consultant to accomplish needs to be clear both to the library and to the prospective consultant. Is the library looking for a full-scale security audit, a written proposal, or just one piece of the overall security pie (such as security of special collections)? The list of expectations for the consultant must be clear before the potential consultants are approached. Not only will a clear list of expectations aid in the bidding and hiring process, such a list will help the prospective consultants determine the correct fee for the project. Legal advice will be necessary for all phases of this engagement process.

COMMERCIAL VENDOR

Commercial vendors are used notably for electronic book-theft-detection systems, surveillance systems, and contract security. Commercial vendors for these assignments are not difficult to find. The use of commercial vendors is often regulated by the institution's guidelines for vendors. Institutions may require that commercial vendors complete a formal bid process. Selection and payment processes may include purchase orders. Legal guidelines for the parent institution must be followed in establishing a relationship with a commercial vendor.

Book-Theft-Detection Systems

Book-theft-detection systems are one specific type of electronic security. Selection of this option should be based on the library's budget, annual losses, long-range goals, and philosophy of service. The plan for what to do if someone is stopped by the electronic book-theft-detection system must be decided before investing in such a system. Aspects of electronic book-theft-detection systems and their operation that impact legal matters include:

- How the system works
- What the system will do
- What is necessary to install it
- Specific features of the system

Decisions about using an electronic book-theft-detection system and about how it will be used should be arranged with legal representation. If a library plans to take action, those actions should have internal administrative and local legal approval. If, however, a library intends to take no action, an electronic book-theft-detection system represents an unnecessary expenditure of library funds.

Surveillance Systems

Electronic surveillance systems may be used at entrances, exits, hard-to-see places, rest rooms, and special collections. Such systems also may be used for fire protection and suppression, intrusion detection, and access controls. (Layne, 1997: 48) Legal issues to consider in the selection of surveillance systems are the same as for electronic book-theft-detection systems and for other commercial vendors. Again, before a system is purchased, the library must know what action it will take when the system works.

Contract Security

Human surveillance may take the form of stationary guards or patrolling guards. Guards may be police, cadets, student assistants, volunteers, or members of a Friends organization. Each type of employee has its own legal and hiring requirements, and each has the clearly defined legal jurisdiction to perform certain tasks, such as detaining, interrogating, or arresting a person. An attorney can differentiate the tasks that are possible for each type of employee according to the laws of the state. Issues of liability relative to contract security should be clearly stated in accordance with the governing regulations for the library or its parent institution.

Service Agreements

Service agreements may be an important part of deciding which system to purchase or of negotiating a purchase contract. Service agreements may be standardized within a vendor organization, but they can vary considerably from vendor to vendor. Also, the library and the parent institution normally have strict service agreement guidelines. Both vendor and library guidelines must be acknowledged. However, there are several basic points to consider in evaluating a service agreement plan. These points include:

- Components of the actual agreement
- Long-term cost
- Additional benefits received
- Vendor performance based on reference checks
- Reliability of the system
- Reliability of the service
- Timeliness of the service (Layne, 1997: 48)

To evaluate service agreement plans, it is wise to consider the service agreement both as a part of the overall system purchase package and as an entity separate from the system package. Using this approach allows greater objectivity in purchasing both the system and the service agreement. In addition, this dual approach allows the components of the system to be priced out separately from the service agreement.

SUMMARY

Each library has a legal obligation to do whatever it can to keep patrons and staff safe in and around the library. The library's efforts should be well documented and should be posted for the public. Further, staff should be well aware of the library's plans for safety. Staff should receive copies of the written safety plans. Library administrators should provide refresher courses for seasoned employees and should mandate specific safety training as a part of the orientation process for new employees.

Planning is the key to success. Libraries should plan for the most likely events in their area. For example, in addition to planning for fire and flooding, libraries in coastal areas should plan for hurricanes. Sometimes safety planning involves considering building evacuations and issues of safe shelter. Development of evacuation routes should be performed in conjunction with police, fire, and ambulance services. The supervisory personnel representing these agencies should get to know the layout of the library; they should be given tours; they should assist in locating and stocking safe shelters. Also, these agencies could be asked to provide training sessions for the library. Finally, they should be asked to keep the library safety officials informed of local activities that might impact the library's security and safety. (Layne, 1997: 50)

In order to meet legal expectations for safety and security management, the library should consider the following suggestions for minimizing liability. (Shuman, 1997: 68–70) Legally the library may be required to:

- Inform library staff of security and safety risks relative to their employment
- Do whatever is reasonable to minimize the safety and security risks to staff and users
- Provide a firm and rapid response to problems of security or safety
- Encourage calm behavior throughout a problem period
- Provide drills for evacuation and other safety and security concerns
- Maintain a telephone tree to alert staff throughout the organization of a problem situation
- Define the role of the security guards and ensure that they perform these roles both in daily interactions and in matters of safety and security
- Provide an annual simulation of emergency situations and their appropriate responses
- Provide in the new employee orientation a thorough training in security and safety measures
- Have a written plan for employees who miss the annual training sessions or the routine drills

Legal issues embracing library security and safety take many forms. This chapter has placed legal issues in the context of local, state, and federal laws, amendments, and interpretations. Since these interpretations may be in a constant state of flux, only general references have been made to the magnitude of legal considerations that apply to the topic of safety and security. The chapter covered legal issues related to formulating an overall security plan, what to do when the plan works, ownership, and probable cause topics. Personnel matters were also discussed. The chapter concluded with references to legal issues regarding consultants, contract security, and electronic systems and their service agreements. Readers are frequently admonished to seek legal advice. Only with real legal advice can the library be certain that it is in compliance with these laws on a daily basis.

REFERENCES

Bassman, Emily S. 1992. *Abuse in the Workplace: Management Remedies and Bottom Line Impact*. Westport, Conn.: Quorum Books.

Bielefield, Arlene, and Lawrence Cheeseman. 1993. *Library Employment within the Law*. New York: Neal-Schuman.

Bintliff, Barbara, and Al Coco. 1984. "Legal Aspects of Library Security." In *Security for Libraries: People, Buildings, Collections*, edited by Marvine Brand. Chicago: American Library Association.

Clark, Edward F. 1998. "Law Enforcement and the Library." In *Management of Library and Archival Security: From the Outside Looking In*, edited by Robert K. O'Neill. New York: Haworth.

Elder, James G. 1986. "Emergency Planning for College and University Libraries." In *Crime Prevention, Security and Emergency Procedures for University Libraries*. Louisville, Ky.: Campus Crime Prevention Programs.

George, Susan C., ed. 1994. *Emergency Planning and Management in College Libraries, CLIP Note #17*. Chicago: American Library Association.

Harold, Victor. 1989. "Loss Prevention Checklists." In *Handbook of Loss Prevention and Crime Prevention*, 2d ed., edited by Lawrence J. Fennelly. Boston: Butterworths.

Layne, Stevan P. 1994a. *The Official Library Security Manual*. Dillon, Co.: Layne Consultants International.

———. 1994b. *Violence in the Library: Prevention, Preparedness and Response*. Dillon, Co.: Layne Consultants International.

———. 1997. "Same Story . . . Different Day." *Library & Archival Security*, 14, no. 1: 45–51.

Lincoln, Alan Jay. 1984. *Crime in the Library: A Study of Patterns, Impact, and Security*. New York: Bowker.

Mason-Robinson, Sally. 1996. *Developing and Managing Video Collections: A How-To-Do-It Manual for Librarians*. New York: Neal-Schuman.

Purpura, Philip P. 1989. "Applicant Screening." In *Handbook of Loss Prevention and Crime Prevention*, 2d ed., edited by Lawrence J. Fennelly. Boston: Butterworths.

Robison, Carolyn L., John D. Marshall, Jr., and Pamela J. Cravey. 1992. "Legal and Practical Aspects of Securing the General Collection in Academic Libraries." In *Academic Libraries in Urban and*

Metropolitan Areas: A Management Handbook, edited by Gerard B. McCabe. New York: Greenwood Press.

Seedman, Albert A. 1989. "Retail Security." In *Handbook of Loss Prevention and Crime Prevention*, 2d ed., edited by Lawrence J. Fennelly. Boston: Butterworths.

Shuman, Bruce A. 1997. "The Devious, the Distraught and the Deranged: Designing and Applying Personal Safety into Library Protection." *Library & Archival Security* 14, no. 1: 53–73.

———. 1999. *Library Security and Safety Handbook: Prevention, Policies, and Procedures*. Chicago: American Library Association.

Switzer, Teri R. 1999. *Safe at Work? Library Security and Safety Issues*. Lanham, Md.: Scarecrow.

CONCLUSION

Eynsham is one of the oldest villages in England. It was built slightly above a floodplain of the Thames River. Close by was the shallowest point on the river, where it was possible for herders to cross, or ford, their pigs. Locally, and for obvious reasons, the area became known as Swinford or Swineford. In 1005 an abbey was begun at Swinford; Aelfric was named its first Abbot. It is likely that this Aelfric, Abbot of Eynsham, is also the infamous Abbot of Swinford who is credited with first unchaining items from the abbey library. (Russell, 1995: 1)

Aelfric also had a record of making knowledge available to the people. Known variously as "the Grammarian" or "Grammaticus," this Aelfric was a prolific writer. His output included homilies written in the spoken Middle English, rather than in the erudite Latin. A contemporary psychological profiler would agree that Aelfric easily could have been the first person to unchain the abbey books so they could be made available. Whether this Aelfric was really the mystical Abbot of Swinford remains a mystery still. Was he responsible for unchaining the first abbey manuscript? Is this tale a part of library lore? Regardless, I like to think of Aelfric as an early leader, a role model in trying to balance access to materials with security of materials.

Of course, in Aelfric's times, security of materials was not complicated. A simple "hex" was usually all that was necessary to assure compliance! Today, however, library security is an enormous and costly endeavor. Done correctly, a comprehensive security program includes:

- An environmental scan, a security audit, and/or a risk analysis to determine the library's assets and vulnerabilities and to monitor the impact of various intervention strategies. (These analyses should occur once and then be reevaluated regularly.)
- An awareness of federal, state, and local laws, statutes, ordinances, and applications relative to security of buildings, users, collections, and digital files. (Libraries must work within the established context of the parent institution to ensure that the appropriate jurisdictional codes are incorporated into the security program.)
- An overall security plan designed to match available security solutions to current security needs for each individual library. (The security plan should be flexible and institution-specific. It should reflect the needs of the insuring arm of the institution. It should also link to the library's formal disaster plan.)
- The identification and empowerment of appropriate people to manage the program. (For example, systems experts may be assigned the security of informational and data files. Archivists may be responsible for the library-wide disaster preparedness and implementation programs. A public services librarian may

be assigned the responsibility for the physical space and protection of a variety of other collections.)

- A process for selecting employees. (When such a program is in place, the best people for each position are selected from a pool of carefully screened applicants.)
- Training for employees and users so they understand security, the security plan, and its ramifications.

"Security" should be treated as one of the core values in the library's mission statement. Data, information, equipment, collections, exhibits, buildings, users, and employees will always require security. Despite its importance as a part of our overall service package, library security seems to be out of fashion right now. For example, at a recent Association of College and Research Libraries national meeting, a series of roundtable discussions was held. A large ballroom was arranged with round dining tables that could each seat ten discussants. Each table featured a different topic. Topics ranged from Electronic Data Interchange (EDI) to electronic sources, from training for off-site library access to building renovation. Only one session was offered on library security—it was advertised as a session on the security audit and security plan. In this very large room full of hundreds of librarians, not one person attended the session on security. One librarian, who serves on the cutting edge of electronic information provision, remarked that she guessed no one was interested in security anymore; she commented on how other topics were more appealing. (This person also represents a large bibliographic utility that is on the leading edge of preservation activities, and she added, "That's too bad.")

Much of my career has been spent working in a metropolitan area at a large university library where multicultural diversity is embraced. We welcomed eligible international students as employees. However, we were always startled when we first met them and they described their awe at our system of casual access to so many library materials. They touched even the rattiest looking books lovingly. They related amazing stories of what they had to do to obtain research information as they pursued their education in their native countries. These storytellers represented the educated men and women of their respective countries. Their tales were not meant to show any disrespect to the resources of their villages. Instead, the stories were vignettes. The students were risking sharing something very personal to show us how much they treasured the chance to shelve books—to immerse themselves in our book-based culture. While it was not part of their plan, these students reminded us about the resourcefulness of the human spirit to find answers, to learn, and to grow. We treasured these encounters because they helped us remember how very lucky we are to be in a free and open environment.

In other cultures, even today, few substantial libraries exist, access to the ones that do exist is limited, and borrowing materials is generally prohibited. Unfortunately, in our fast-paced culture, we have come to take our bibliographic largesse, and our access to the materials, for granted. In fact, we seem now to have taken what was once a privilege to be a right. Libraries strive for a welcoming attitude, we are open to all, and we are glad to serve. We especially relish the opportunity to serve the underserved. We provide open stack collections, shelved in a largely unsupervised labyrinth. We offer materials in a variety of formats—some easily able to be slipped into a pocket or purse. We have information that represents a broad view of subject matter. In fact, our knowledge vat is so vast that attracting opponents and proponents of any topic is likely. As librarians, we realize that access to information and the right to interpret it in personal ways is the bedrock of a democracy (Hessel, 1955: 100). To that end, we also offer a wide range of government publications, which, by contract, must be available to anyone who wishes to use them.

The idea in our society of the library building as a safe haven is diminishing. Two of the reasons for this change in perception are the reported increases in theft and mutilation of library materials, and a documented change in the attitudes of people in public places. Shootings, physical assaults, and verbal threats represent only some of the attacks on "self" that people have come to fear in public places. Among the consequences of the change in public opinion about safety in public places, including libraries, are increases in tension, anger, and fear. These emotions are cyclical. As they increase, they generate additional tension, anger, and fear. Thus, the cycle escalates. The reality is, only with a lot of effort can we make these public buildings safe.

In many discussions of the library of the future, the traditional print-based library is portrayed as old-fashioned, dated, and out-of-favor because users are forced to comply with opening hours, user regulations, and policies developed to ensure the safety of physical collections. As we move toward the library of the future, we must keep in mind that security should remain an integral part of the overall service package we offer. We offer this package, not because we are rigid and opposed to change, but because we are entrusted with preserving materials, assuring access to materials, and offering availability of materials in a timely fashion. Is a plate that has been torn from an art folio any more or less important than an electronic journal article that is unavailable because of a power outage? Is a virtual library shut down by security breaches any better than a traditional library infested with flashers and thieves?

Instead of seeing libraries as "old" or "new," "traditional" or "modern," we should look at the library as being in the process of continuous change and renewal. The "renewed library is one that is ever-evolving and continuously striving to fully satisfy the needs of all those who influence and are influenced by it." (Carson, Carson, and Phillips, 1997: 8) At the beginning of this book, the security breaches of theft and mutilation were described as violations of the spirit of the library, as attacks on our very culture. In a sociological sense, the first general societal function of libraries is "the maintenance of culture through maintenance of access to knowledge records. In a general sense, it is the importance of this function that legitimates the authority of librarianship. . . ." (Winter, 1988: 77)

Security should be an integral part of a library's overall service package. In a sociological sense, the format of our knowledge records is insignificant. Securing them and their users is the critical point. A successful security program reflects the following attributes:

- Planning
- Assessing the situation
- Attacking the issues
- Protecting users, buildings, collections, electronics
- Writing
- Collaborating
- Training

Protecting Library Staff, Users, Collections, and Facilities has provided a framework for developing a relevant and evolving security program for any size and type of library. As society changes, the need will remain for people to feel physically secure as they pursue their learning adventure. Library security in the traditional, new, or renewed library should be like the four-year-old family dog. It is always taking care of you, but you don't think of it primarily as a security system. You can enjoy your life in different ways, and you sleep more securely at night because it is there. Library security does not just happen. It takes lots of effort on the part of library employees to make it work. When it works, it is like the Olympic gymnast who can make the release moves on the uneven bars look effortless. A lot of background preparation has gone into the routine, but what the audience sees is how it is so very fluid and integrated. What then is library security? It is the end result of surveying, brainstorming, listening, planning, and preparing all that goes into ensuring that visits to the library are routine!

REFERENCES

Carson, Kerry David, Paula Phillips Carson, and Joyce Schouest Phillips. 1997. *The ABCs of Collaborative Change: The Manager's Guide to Library Renewal.* Chicago: American Library Association.

Hessel, Alfred. 1955. *A History of Libraries.* Translated by Reuben Peiss. New Brunswick, N.J.: Scarecrow.

Russell, Ralph E. 1995. "The Trustee/Director Role in a Library Network." *Advances in Library Administration and Organization* 13: 1–9.

Winter, Michael F. 1988. *The Culture and Control of Expertise: Toward a Sociological Understanding of Librarianship.* New York: Greenwood Press.

INDEX

A

Access (to)
    building, 2, 9, 10, 13, 18, 27, 42, 53, 56,
        126, 128, 134, 156, 167
    information, 27, 28–29, 42, 111, 165, 167–
        168
Access management, 3, 9, 10, 19, 28, 46, 56,
    75, 109
Accidents, 5, 6, 117
Addict, 5, 6, 8, 63, 137
Aggression, 63, 69
Air quality, 5, 6, 60
Alarms, 2, 6, 7, 9, 10, 14, 36, 44–46, 54–55,
    61, 101, 109, 114, 117, 141–143, 145
Amnesty days, 30, 39
Annunciation systems. *see* Alarms
Arrest, 35, 37, 136, 143, 153–154. *see also*
    Prosecution
Arson. *see* Natural disasters
Assaults, 3, 8, 137, 167
Availability (in computing security), 79, 87, 101

B

Background checks. *see* Preemployment
    screening
Bid process, 157–158
Bites and stings, 5, 6
Body fluids, 62
Bombs and bomb threats, 5–7, 20, 55, 59, 62–
    63
Book returns and drops, 2, 10, 14, 18, 55–56
Building takeover, 5, 6, 10, 13

C

Census (statistical technique), 33
Change machine, 4, 9

Checklist, 12, 147–149
Checkroom, 39–40
Closed circuit television (CCTV), 3, 7, 46, 75
Closed stacks, 3, 28, 40, 109
Concealment, 139–141
Confidentiality, 79–80, 87, 101, 119, 134, 137,
    150
Consultant, security, 12, 157–158
Conventions. *see* Special events
Court, 37, 115, 136, 143–144, 147
Credit checks. *see* Preemployment screening
Crimes of opportunity, 1, 3
Criminal background tests. *see* Preemployment
    screening
Criminal Trespass Warning, 37–38, 70
Custodial services, 10, 19, 32, 60, 107–108,
    116

D

Demonstrations. *see* Special events
Digitizing, 40, 42
Disaster preparedness, 6, 9, 20, 22, 58–63, 87,
    114–118, 165
Discipline, 154–155
Documentation (of security cases), 143–149
Door guards, 43–44, 47
Doors, 2, 7, 9, 13–14, 54– 56, 75
Drinking, 4, 54, 58, 68, 113
Drug problem. *see* Addict
Drug testing. *see* Preemployment screening

E

Earthquake. *see* Natural disasters
Eating, 4, 54, 58, 66, 68, 113
Electronic book-theft-detection system, 9, 36,
    44–45, 53, 61, 63, 136, 139, 141–143, 145,
    158–159

Elevator, 2, 5–6, 20
Emergency, 4–5, 7, 52, 62, 64
Emergency exit, 7, 10, 13, 56
Emergency preparedness. *see* Disaster preparedness
Employment. *see* Hiring
Environment, 59, 60–61, 105–106, 153
Environmental scan, 53–54, 165
Escort service, 3, 55
Ethics, 99–100
Evacuation, 2, 55, 59–63, 117, 160
Evaluation, performance, 100, 154
Evidence, 41, 115, 140–141, 144–148
Exhibitionism, 3, 8, 20, 63
Exhibits, 14, 105–106, 118, 166

F

False alarm, 15, 37, 61, 141–143
False imprisonment, 133
Fingerprint technology, 75
Fire. *see* Natural disasters
First aid kit, 7, 62
First offender, 37, 146–148
Flood. *see* Natural disasters
Floor plans, 7, 12, 107, 109
Food. *see* Eating
Fourteenth Amendment, 133–135
Fourth Amendment, 133
Fund raising, 38, 47, 75

G

Gangs, 3
Gloves (protective), 52, 62, 140

H

Handwriting analysis. *see* Preemployment screening
Harassment, 6, 20–22, 45, 52, 69–70, 131
Hex, 165
Hiring, 65, 119, 150–152, 156, 166. *see also* Preemployment screening
Hours (of operation), 3, 28, 39, 126, 128, 147
Hurricane. *see* Natural disasters

I

Identification, 10, 19, 42, 46–47, 56, 70, 89, 99, 109, 111, 126–128, 146
Insurance, 10, 12, 89, 113, 115, 118–119, 131, 157
Integrity (in computing security), 79, 80, 87, 101
Intercom systems, 7, 57

Internet, 51, 71, 96–99, 107, 109
Intrusion detection system. *see* alarms
Inventory, 9, 13, 19, 30, 32–33, 88–89, 92, 114–115, 119

J

Juveniles, 146, 148

K

Keys, 2, 10, 13, 15, 19, 32, 41, 54, 56–57, 92, 107–108, 112–113, 126, 141, 155–156

L

Landscaping, 2, 54–56
Laws. *see* Legal issues
Legal counsel, 8, 10, 115
Legal issues, 30, 35, 36–38, 45, 57, 61–62, 65–66, 68–69, 73–74, 76, 99–101, 110, 119, 120, 131–162, 165. *see also* Student judiciary
Library security officer (LSO), 110–111, 114
Licensing agreements, 43, 86, 94, 97, 100, 157
Lie detector test, *see* Preemployment screening
Lighting, 2, 7, 9, 10, 18, 54–55, 57
Local ordinances, *see* Laws
Lockers, 20, 41, 154
Locks, 2, 7, 10, 13–14, 19, 20, 41, 54, 56, 107, 109, 112, 126, 155–156
Loiterer, 63, 68
Loss rate, 32–33, 47
Lost item (defined), 29–30

M

Manuals, 10, 11, 136–138
Mirror, 43, 47
Missing item (defined), 29–30
Monitor. *see* patrol
Motion detector, 55, 114
Mutilation (of item), 4, 7, 13, 27–29, 31–32, 37, 41, 46, 68, 115, 131, 136, 139–141, 143, 145, 167, 169
Mutilation rate. *see* Loss rate

N

Naming conventions for computer hardware, 88–89
Natural disasters, 3–8, 14, 53, 59–61, 106, 116–117

O

Offsite storage of data, 9, 15, 91, 92–93

Olympics and Para-Olympics. *see* Special events

Overdue item, 7, 29–30, 131

P

Paging equipment, 7, 20,

Parking lot, 2, 7, 9–10, 18, 54–55

Password. *see* Security (of) password

Patrol, 3, 10, 36–37, 45, 54, 57, 74

Patron behavior (problem), 3, 5–8, 63–64, 67, 131

Personnel, 36, 38, 43, 45, 55, 71, 74, 76, 85, 133, 138, 150–156, 159

Photocopy, 4, 11, 41, 109, 113, 141, 146

Police, 8, 20, 36, 38, 45, 70, 74, 115
    beat office in the library, 20, 37
    security risk, 108

Policies and procedures, 3–4, 7, 9–10, 13, 20–22, 32, 36, 38, 43, 45, 64, 66–72, 76, 80, 85, 96–99, 106, 110–112, 118, 132, 134–137, 152–155, 167

Political conventions. *see* Special events

Polygraph test. *see* Preemployment screening

Portable computing environment, 81–82, 95–96

Power outages, 5, 6, 7

Preemployment screening, 3, 32, 58, 64–66, 112, 131, 150, 151–152

Preservation, 105–106, 108

Privacy. *see* Confidentiality

Probable cause, 31, 133, 138, 140, 143, 148

Property marking, 9–10, 13, 31, 41, 88, 107, 112–113, 115, 119, 131, 138–139

Prosecution, 115, 132–133, 155. *see also* Arrest

Proximity card. *see* Radio Frequency Identification (RF-ID)

Psychiatric problems, 5, 6

Publicity. *see* Signage

R

Radio-Frequency Identification (RF-ID), 46, 56, 75

Rare Books and Manuscripts Section (RBMS), 111–113, 115, 120

Reports, 115, 136, 144–149

Rest rooms, 2, 7, 52, 54–57, 140, 143, 159

Risk management (for computing security), 21, 82, 87–96, 98, 101, 165

Robotics, 46–47

Role playing, 45, 72, 132

S

Safeguards (in computing security), 79, 81–82

Safety. *see* Security

Sampling (statistical technique), 13, 33

Search, 38, 133, 136, 140, 145

Security (of),
    audio-visuals, 4
    building, 1–3, 9–11, 35, 53–58, 76, 165–166, 169
    collections, 9, 27–47, 76, 131, 135, 165, 166, 168
    computer hardware and software, 79, 81–82, 86, 93–94
    data, 21, 79, 81, 82–86, 94, 131 165–166, 168
    equipment, 4, 7, 9, 29, 79, 105, 166, 168
    information, 1, 4, 9, 29, 79, 82–86, 100, 143, 165, 166
    money, 3, 9, 19
    non-print collections, 4, 9, 139
    password, 9, 15, 155–156
    people, 1, 2–3, 9, 10, 51–77, 105, 109, 117, 131, 136, 160, 165, 166, 168
    special collections, 4, 13, 14, 105–120, 159
    supplies, 92–93

Security, appearance of, 40, 42, 43, 47, 56, 74

Security, electronic, 79–101

Security audit, 1, 11–22, 110, 158, 165
    benefits, 22–23
    definition, 12
    development of, 15–16
    examples of, 12–15
    report, 12, 16, 17–22

Security guards, 7, 13, 38, 43, 45, 55, 56, 74, 128, 133–134, 158–159, 161

Security issues (breadth of/scope), 1–11

Security plan, 1, 47, 110–114, 126–127, 132–133, 134, 128, 158, 165

Security proposal, 34–35, 38, 39, 47, 132

Security solutions, 39–47

Service agreement, 36, 44, 160

Sexual activity, 3, 6, 54, 63, 68

Sight lines, 54, 58

Signage, 2, 38, 70, 71, 76, 99, 137–138, 141, 160

Smoking, 4, 54, 58, 68, 113

Special events, 123–129

Sporting events. *see* Special events

Stairwell, 2, 54, 57, 61, 140

Stings. *see* Bites and stings

Stolen item (defined), 29–31

Storage, 9, 10, 19, 42, 46, 57, 92, 106, 114, 143

Student judiciary, 37, 144, 146

Surprise (as an element of security), 123–124, 127, 129

Surveillance, 10, 19, 57, 66, 75, 114, 131, 134, 158–159

Survey, 11, 15–16

T

Telephone (emergency), 3, 7, 10, 45, 55, 57, 127

Telephone security, 3, 75

Telephone tree, 117, 161

Temperature (building), 60, 114

Termination (of employment), 3, 11, 13, 113, 155–156

Theft, 3, 4, 5, 7, 8, 13, 27–29, 30, 37, 115, 120, 136, 167– 168
   definition, 31
   employee, 32, 65, 92, 107–108, 150, 153, 156

Theft by conversion (legal term), 30

Theft by taking (legal term), 31

Threats, 3, 69, 73

Tornado. *see* Natural disasters

Training, 6–9, 20–21, 36–37, 45, 47, 70, 72–76, 82, 113–114, 116, 118–119, 137–138, 153, 160–161, 166, 168

Trash cans, 79, 81, 140

V

Vagrants, 3, 8

Vandalism, 6, 8, 13–14, 27, 45, 68

Vending machine, 9, 58

Vendors, 12, 44, 71, 157–159

Vermin. *see* Natural disasters

Video simulations. *see* Preemployment screening

Violence, 6, 27, 71, 73, 131, 150, 156

Voyeurism, 3, 20, 70

Vulnerabilities, 10, 53–58, 79, 81, 88, 93, 101

W

Water problems (leaks, drips, mains), 5, 6, 116

Weapons 68, 69, 72, 133

Weather emergencies. *see* Natural disasters

Wind. *see* Natural disasters

Windows, 14, 54, 56, 116

Workplace violence. *see* Violence

ABOUT THE AUTHOR

Pamela J. Cravey, Ph.D., is an independent librarian consultant who specializes in materials management, administrative planning, and research. Her career in public service and library management has spanned thirty years in four large academic libraries. Recently retired as Associate Professor (*Emerita*) and Head of the Access Services Department at Pullen Library, Georgia State University, Atlanta. She is grateful to all the staff of the Department who understood the importance of library security and who worked so diligently to preserve the spirit of the library while still protecting the rights of the patrons.